LUNCHBOX
SALADS

EBURY
PRESS

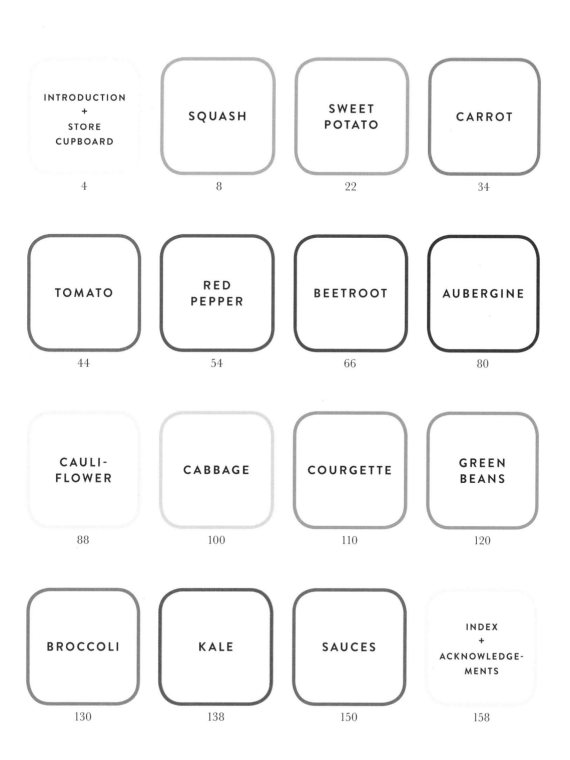

INTRODUCTION

HEY

We're two cooks who love all food and enjoy eating healthily for the way it makes us feel.

After training and working as chefs and in the food industry in London and abroad, a few years ago we decided to start a food delivery business in London called Lunch BXD. We felt that so much 'healthy' food was restrictive or dull and we wanted to show how it could be zingy, filling and flavoursome, and naturally healthy too. Each morning we prepared lunchboxes and then hopped on our bicycles to deliver them to offices around the city. It was a whirlwind adventure of quinoa, kale and our signature satay sauce.

This book contains everything we learned along the way about making fast, fresh and simple good food. We want to show you that salad can be much more than just lettuce leaves.

Hope you enjoy.

Naomi Twigden and Anna Pinder
@bxdideas

HOW THIS BOOK WORKS

The aim of this book is to offer easy, approachable, affordable, convenient, substantial AND vibrant salad inspiration for every working day. All the recipes here use 10 or fewer easy-to-buy ingredients and take no more than 30 minutes to make.

Our salads are substantial portions designed to keep your energy levels up throughout the afternoon. Every recipe makes 2 portions and everything will keep well for 2 days in the fridge. (We've included specific packing instructions with each recipes to avoid soggy leaves at lunchtime.)

We sometimes suggest packing the dressing separately. To do this, line a mug or glass with 2 pieces of clingfilm. Make sure you have a good bit extra hanging over the sides of the mug/glass on all sides, then pour in the dressing or dip. Gather the extra clingfilm and twist into a knot to seal the dressing inside. Pop the clingfilm pouch into your lunchbox or bag. When you are ready to serve, pierce the clingfilm with a fork or knife and pour the dressing out.

The recipes are designed to be cost-effective and repeat ingredients in different ways so you don't end up with lots of waste or a larder full of different spices and grains. There's a suggested list of store cupboard ingredients on page 7, which are used throughout this book. There is also an index on page 158, listing where every ingredient is used to help you make the best of any leftovers.

This is not a vegetarian cookbook but each chapter in this book is focused around a hero vegetable. They are our heroes because they are either the largest element of the dish or the star in terms of flavour. You'll find meat and fish ideas here too but we want to celebrate the versatility of veg, and break the misconception that you need meat and fish to make a meal.

Using vegetables over meat and fish cuts down costs – if you're making packed lunches you're probably aiming to save money, so by focusing on vegetables that's a lot easier to do.

By focusing on one main vegetable it is easier to find a recipe that uses up what is available and limits food waste too.

There's a lot in the press about why eating less meat is good for our health and the environment. We personally feel better on a balanced, colourful diet packed full of fresh vegetables.

Our recipes are easy to customise, though, to suit your taste buds or dietary preferences. Feel free to add chicken or swap cheese for tofu.

The recipes are your basic guide but cooking them should be creative and fun, so we've added tips throughout the book to help you get creative in the kitchen and use up what you have in the fridge or what is in season.

STORE CUPBOARD

All our recipes have 10 ingredients or fewer and assume you already own oil, salt and pepper. To help keep costs down and minimise waste, the following ingredients would be handy to have in stock as they appear frequently throughout the book.

CANNED/JARRED
Chickpeas
Sweetcorn
Tuna
Kidney beans
Butter beans
Jarred roasted red peppers

SAUCES
Cider vinegar (or balsamic or white wine)
Soy sauce
Peanut butter (preferably sugar-free)
Runny honey or brown sugar
Harissa
Tahini

DRY STORE
Unsalted cashews
Flaked almonds
Pumpkin seeds
Sesame seeds
Desiccated coconut

GRAINS
Brown rice/wild rice
Puy lentils
Wholewheat pasta
Quinoa
Dry noodles

SPICES
Ground cumin
Dried chilli flakes
Ground cinnamon
Smoked paprika
Dried Italian herbs
Curry powder

FRESH/FROZEN
Lemons/limes
Garlic
Ginger
Frozen peas
Frozen shelled edamame beans
Greek yoghurt

We specify different nuts, seeds and pasta types in our recipes for variety and flavour but all types would work well.

UTENSILS
All recipes are easy to make with basic cooking equipment. A blender is required for some recipes as is a spiraliser. If you don't have a spiraliser, vegetables can often be bought pre-spiralised or you can shave them into ribbons with a peeler instead.

OILS
We recommend different oils based on the flavour or how they work at high temperatures but they are mostly interchangeable – in general we use mild olive oil for drizzling and dressing and rapeseed oil or coconut oil for cooking.

SQUASH NOODLES WITH PRAWNS + COCONUT-LIME DRESSING

INGREDIENTS:

150g frozen shelled edamame beans
$^1\!/_2$ large butternut squash (the thinner
   part with no seeds)
coconut oil
2 handfuls of raw peeled prawns
2 red peppers
2 portions of Coconut-lime Dressing
   (see page 153)

TRY THIS...

Swap the coconut dressing for another, such
as one of our pestos/Satay Dressing/Peanut
Teriyaki Sauce *(see pages 154–156).*

METHOD:

Put the edamame in a bowl of cold water and
set aside to thaw.

Peel the squash and spiralise into noodles
(or grate/shave with a peeler). Place in a frying
pan with 2 teaspoons of coconut oil and fry over
a medium-high heat for 4–5 minutes until just
cooked through and slightly crisp. Keep stirring.
Remove the squash from the pan with a slotted
spoon and set aside in a bowl.

Add the prawns to the same pan with a little
more coconut oil and fry over a high heat for
about 2 minutes until pink. Add to the squash
and allow to cool.

Meanwhile, remove the core and seeds from the
red peppers, then cut into thin strips. Drain the
edamame. Add the peppers and edamame to
the squash and prawns and toss together. Season
with salt and pepper.

To pack: Spoon the salad into two lunchboxes.
Pack the dressing separately.

ROAST DUKKAH SQUASH + KALE WITH RICOTTA

INGREDIENTS:

1 butternut squash
olive oil
150g chopped kale
20 fresh mint/coriander leaves
lime juice
80g ricotta (or feta)

Dukkah
1 teaspoon ground coriander and/or cumin
1 handful of sesame seeds
1 handful of mixed nuts (flaked almonds/
   pistachios/hazelnuts work well, or a
   combination)

TRY THIS…

· Add a 400g can of sweetcorn or chickpeas,
  drained and rinsed.

· Try the dukkah on poached eggs and avocado
  at breakfast.

METHOD:

Preheat the oven to 180°C and boil a full
kettle. Peel the squash and cut into large chunks,
discarding the seeds. Place in a pan with a pinch
of salt and cover with boiled water. Boil for
5 minutes until just soft.

Drain and place on a baking tray with a little
oil and seasoning. Roast for 15–20 minutes until
golden brown and slightly crisp. Turn the chunks
every few minutes.

While the squash is being prepared, place the
chopped kale in a bowl, cover with boiled water
and add a pinch of salt. Leave for 5 minutes,
then drain and rinse under cold water.

Toast the dukkah spices in a dry frying pan over
a medium heat, stirring all the time, for 1 minute
until fragrant. Add the sesame seeds and nuts,
and stir until browned. Blitz in a food processor,
or pound using a pestle and mortar, until
roughly ground.

Add the kale to the squash and mix the dukkah
through along with the torn mint or coriander
leaves, a little olive oil, lime juice to taste
and seasoning.

To pack: Spoon the salad into two lunchboxes and
dot the ricotta on top.

TIP: Dukkah is an Egyptian spice blend. Make a bigger batch – it will keep for weeks stored in
an airtight container – because it makes a great crunchy topper for any simple salad.

ROAST ROOT VEGETABLES WITH AVOCADO, FETA + PEA DIP

INGREDIENTS:

1 small butternut squash
2 red onions
2 carrots
coconut/olive oil
50g baby spinach leaves

Dip
2 handfuls of frozen peas
1 avocado
30g feta
15 fresh mint leaves
lemon juice

TRY THIS...

· Swap the peas for a handful of frozen shelled
  edamame beans, thawed in a bowl of cold
  water for 1–2 minutes, or canned butter beans,
  drained and rinsed.

· Bake a chicken breast with the vegetables for
  the final 15 minutes. Shred the chicken, using
  two forks to pull the meat apart.

· Make extra dip and serve on toast at breakfast
  with tomatoes and crisp-fried chorizo.

METHOD:

Preheat the oven to 200°C and boil a full kettle.
Peel the squash, red onions and carrots and cut
into 2cm chunks, discarding the squash seeds.

Place the squash in a pan, cover with boiled
water and add a pinch of salt. Simmer for
2 minutes. Add the carrots and onion and
simmer for another 2 minutes. Drain the
vegetables and spread out on a baking tray.
Drizzle over a little oil and season. Mix together.
Roast for 25 minutes until cooked through and
crisp. Stir every few minutes. Cool.

While the vegetables are roasting, thaw the
peas in a bowl of cold water for 1–2 minutes;
drain. Scoop the flesh from the avocado into a
food processor and add the feta, mint and peas.
Blitz briefly (it should be chunky). Season, adding
lemon juice to taste and as much water/oil as
you need to loosen to a dip-like consistency.

To pack: Once the roasted vegetables are cool,
toss through the spinach, then spoon into the
lunchboxes. Pack the dip separately.

CRUNCHY SQUASH SATAY SALAD

INGREDIENTS:

1 small butternut squash
coconut/olive oil
120g quinoa
½ red cabbage
1 green pepper
2 portions of Satay Dressing *(see page 156)*

TRY THIS…

· Drizzle oil and honey over a chicken breast
  and sprinkle with some sesame seeds. Bake in
  a 180°C oven for 15–18 minutes. Slice and add
  to the lunchboxes.

· Sprinkle with toasted and lightly crushed
  peanuts for extra crunch.

METHOD:

Preheat the oven to 200°C and boil a full kettle.
Peel the squash and cut into roughly 3cm chunks,
discarding the seeds. Place on a baking tray with
a splash of oil and a pinch of salt. Roast for
15–20 minutes until tender and golden. Halfway
through cooking, give the tray a shake/stir to
prevent the squash chunks from catching.

Meanwhile, put the quinoa in a pan and cover
with boiled water. Cook for 8–10 minutes until
al dente. Drain and rinse under cold water.

While the quinoa cooks, remove the outer leaves
and core from the red cabbage, then thinly slice.
Dice the pepper into small strips, discarding the
core and seeds.

Mix the cabbage and pepper through the quinoa
and season with a pinch of salt. Toss the squash
with the satay dressing.

To pack: Spread the quinoa in two lunchboxes
and pile the squash on top.

JERK CHICKEN + SQUASH WITH QUINOA + PEAS

INGREDIENTS:

1 small butternut squash
2 skinless boneless chicken breasts
100g quinoa
120g frozen peas
2 tablespoons finely chopped fresh coriander
juice of 2 limes

Jerk rub
1½ tablespoons sugar/honey
1½ tablespoons coconut oil
2 tablespoons bought jerk seasoning
   (or 2 teaspoons ground allspice, 1½ teaspoons
   dried thyme/mixed Italian herbs and a good
   pinch of ground cinnamon)

TRY THIS...

· Replace the chicken or quinoa with a 400g can
  of black beans, drained and rinsed/2 handfuls
  of chopped kale, blanched in boiling water for
  5 minutes/1 chopped mango.

· Add a sprinkle of desiccated coconut to the
  chicken and squash for the final 5 minutes
  of cooking, for extra sweetness.

· Use the same rub on chicken thighs or
  drumsticks on a barbecue.

· Replace the jerk rub with Peanut Teriyaki
  Sauce *(see page 156)*.

METHOD:

Preheat the oven to 200°C and boil a full kettle.
Peel the squash and chop into 2cm cubes. Place
in a pan and cover with boiled water. Add a
pinch of salt and cook for 5 minutes. Drain and
spread out on a baking tray with the chicken.

Mix all the jerk rub ingredients together with some
seasoning and use to thoroughly coat the squash
and chicken. Bake for 15–18 minutes until the
chicken is cooked through. Stir every 5 minutes.

Meanwhile, put the quinoa in a pan, cover with
boiled water and add a pinch of salt. Cook for
8–10 minutes until al dente, then drain and rinse
under cold water. Thaw the peas in a bowl of
cold water for 1–2 minutes; drain.

Cut the cooked chicken at an angle into 1–2cm
thick slices. Mix together the quinoa, chicken,
squash, peas, coriander and any juices from the
baking tray. Season and add lime juice to taste.

To pack: Spoon into two lunchboxes.

MOROCCAN SQUASH, GREEN BEANS, APRICOTS + PISTACHIOS

INGREDIENTS:

1 red onion
2cm piece fresh ginger
coconut/olive oil
2 tablespoons ras el hanout (or 1½ teaspoons
    ground cinnamon, 2 teaspoons ground cumin
    and 1½ teaspoons ground coriander)
2 tablespoons tomato purée
1 small butternut squash
160g green beans
8 fresh (or dried) apricots
50g unsalted pistachios (or flaked almonds)

TRY THIS…

· Garnish with picked fresh coriander and a
  drizzle of honey.

· Add sliced chicken to the softened spiced onion
  and fry together until cooked through before
  adding the rest of the ingredients.

· Create a tagine: add a 400g can of chopped
  tomatoes and a 400g can of chickpeas, rinsed
  and drained, after the final 2 minutes of
  cooking. Simmer for 10–15 minutes until
  thickened.

· Create a lamb tagine: add 160–200g diced
  lamb to the softened spiced onion and
  brown well before adding the squash, beans
  and apricots, followed by the tomatoes and
  chickpeas (as above).

METHOD:

Boil a full kettle. Peel and finely dice the onion
and ginger. Place in a pan with a little oil, all the
other spices and the tomato purée. Fry over a low
heat for about 8 minutes until the onion is soft,
stirring occasionally.

Meanwhile, peel the squash and chop into 3cm
pieces, discarding the seeds. Place in a pan with
a little salt and cover with boiled water. Cook for
6–7 minutes. Drain and rinse under cold water.

Trim the green beans and cut in half. Place in
a pan with a pinch of salt and cover with boiled
water. Cook for 3–5 minutes until just tender but
still very crunchy. Drain and rinse under cold water.

Cut the apricots into quarters, discarding the
stones. (If using dried apricots, pour boiled water
over them and leave for 5 minutes to plump up
before draining and roughly dicing.)

Add the squash, beans and apricots to the onions
and cook everything together for 2 minutes.
Keep stirring. Season to taste.

Toast the nuts in a dry pan.

To pack: Allow the squash salad to cool before
spooning into two lunchboxes. Sprinkle the
nuts on top.

SAGE + SQUASH PASTA WITH PARMA HAM, ROCKET + LEMON

INGREDIENTS:

100g wholemeal fusilli
coconut/olive oil
1 small butternut squash
8 fresh sage leaves
100g frozen peas
50g Parmesan
4 slices Parma ham
½ lemon
50g rocket

TRY THIS…

· Swap the Parma ham and Parmesan for
  cooked streaky bacon and Cheddar.

· Stir in a tablespoon of crème fraîche for
  a creamier sauce.

· Add dried/fresh chilli for heat.

· Sprinkle a handful of toasted pine nuts
  over the rocket.

METHOD:

Boil a full kettle. Put the pasta in a pan, cover
with boiled water and add a pinch of salt. Cook
for 12–14 minutes until al dente. Drain the pasta,
keeping back half a ladle of pasta water to add
to the sauce at the end. Mix the pasta with a little
oil to prevent sticking.

While the pasta is cooking, peel the squash and
chop into 2cm cubes, discarding the seeds. Place
in another pan, cover with boiled water and cook
for 5 minutes until just tender. Drain.

Tip the squash into a frying pan and tear over
the sage leaves. Add a little oil and fry over a
medium heat for 5 minutes until golden brown
all over. Meanwhile, thaw the peas in a bowl of
cold water for 1–2 minutes; drain.

Stir the pasta, reserved pasta water and peas
through the squash. Mix well. Zest in the lemon
and season with juice to taste and a good amount
of black pepper.

To pack: Allow to cool, then spoon into two
lunchboxes and pile the rocket on top. Grate
over the Parmesan and top with the roughly
torn Parma ham.

TIP: Adding some of the pasta cooking liquid at the end helps thicken the sauce
as the liquid contains starch from the pasta.

SQUASH NOODLES WITH
PESTO-BAKED CHICKEN

INGREDIENTS:

2 skinless boneless chicken breasts
2 portions of Green Pesto *(see page 154)*
1 small butternut squash
coconut/olive oil
100g frozen peas
1 x 240g can sweetcorn

METHOD:

Preheat the oven to 180°C. Place the chicken on a baking tray. Coat with half the pesto, then bake for 15–18 minutes until cooked through. Cool, then slice at an angle.

While the chicken is in the oven, peel the squash and remove the seeds. Spiralise the bottom, thinner part of the squash (the seeded half won't spiralise) and shave the seeded part into ribbons with a peeler. (If you don't have a spiraliser you can shave the whole squash into ribbons.) Place the squash in a frying pan with a little oil and seasoning. Fry over a high heat for 3–5 minutes until just cooked.

Thaw the peas in a bowl of cold water for 1–2 minutes; drain. Drain the sweetcorn.

To pack: Spoon the peas, sweetcorn and noodles into the lunchboxes. Place the chicken on top and add the remaining pesto.

TRY THIS...

Swap the chicken for 2 trout fillets, baking them for 12 minutes.

TIP:

Having frozen peas on hand makes it easy to bulk out meals with an extra portion of vegetables. If thawed quickly in a bowl of cold water (they don't need cooking), they will keep more of their crunch and colour.

SQUASH, CASHEW + SPINACH SALAD WITH TAHINI DRESSING

INGREDIENTS:

1 red onion
coconut/olive oil
1 small butternut squash
80g unsalted cashews
2 handfuls of pomegranate seeds
50g baby spinach leaves

Dressing
2 teaspoons tahini
2 tablespoons natural yoghurt
1 teaspoon cold-pressed rapeseed oil
1 teaspoon honey
lemon juice

TRY THIS...

Swap the tahini dressing and pomegranate seeds for one of our pestos *(see pages 154–155)* and feta.

METHOD:

Boil a full kettle. Peel and dice the onion. Fry in a pan with a little oil over a low heat for about 10 minutes until soft.

Meanwhile, peel the squash and chop into 2cm chunks, discarding the seeds. Place in a pan with a pinch of salt and cover with boiled water. Cook for 5 minutes until just soft. Drain.

Add the squash and a little more oil to the onion. Turn up the heat and fry for 2–3 minutes until slightly golden. Remove the onion and squash and cool.

Wipe the pan dry. Lightly crush the nuts, then toast in the dry pan for 2 minutes until golden brown.

Whisk the dressing ingredients together with 1 teaspoon water and season.

To pack: Mix the squash and onion with the nuts and spoon into two lunchboxes. Top with the pomegranate seeds and spinach. Pack the dressing separately.

SWEET POTATO

4 IDEAS FOR
SWEET POTATO JACKETS

INGREDIENTS:

2 sweet potatoes
coconut/olive oil
50g baby spinach leaves
plus one of the topping options
   (see opposite and overleaf)

METHOD:

Preheat the oven to 210°C and boil a full kettle.
Cut the unpeeled sweet potatoes lengthways in
half and place in a pan. Cover with boiled water
and add a pinch of salt. Boil for 6–8 minutes
until just cooked through. (Test with a knife in
the centre.) Drain.

Lay the sweet potato halves skin side down on
a baking tray. Drizzle over a little oil and season.
Bake for 20 minutes until slightly crisp. While
they are in the oven, prepare one of the toppings.
(Note that some of the topping elements are
baked with the sweet potatoes.)

To pack: Cool the sweet potatoes (and the topping,
if necessary) before packing. Place the sweet
potato halves side by side in the lunchboxes and
spoon the topping alongside. Pile the spinach on
top or to the side.

Spring onion, Parma ham and chive topping

3 spring onions (white bulbs and most of
  the green)
4 slices Parma ham
3 tablespoons crème fraîche/natural yoghurt
1 tablespoon finely snipped fresh chives

Finely slice the spring onions and Parma ham.

Once the sweet potatoes have been baking for
15 minutes, remove from the oven and scoop out
the flesh into a bowl (leave enough on the skin to
keep the shape). Mix with the topping ingredients,
season, then spoon back into the potato skins.

Return to the oven and bake for a further 5 minutes.

Apple, beetroot and pecan slaw topping (above)

80g pecans
2 apples
3 ready-cooked and peeled beetroots
15 fresh mint leaves
2 tablespoons crème fraîche/natural yoghurt

Roughly chop the pecans and add to the
baking tray with the sweet potatoes for the final
3 minutes of their cooking, to toast the nuts.

Grate the apples and beetroots into a sieve set
over the sink. Use your hands to squeeze out any
excess liquid. Tip into a bowl and fold through
the torn mint leaves. Mix through the crème
fraîche. Stir the toasted pecans through the slaw.

Smoky baked beans topping

1 small white/red onion
1 garlic clove
$\frac{1}{2}$ teaspoon smoked paprika
$\frac{1}{2}$ teaspoon ground cumin
olive oil
$\frac{1}{2}$ x 400g can chopped tomatoes
40g Cheddar
Worcestershire sauce (optional)
1 x 400g can kidney beans
Tabasco (optional)

Peel and finely chop the onion. Peel and crush the garlic. Fry together in a medium pan with the spices and a splash of oil over a low heat for 10 minutes until very soft. Add the tomatoes and stir, then leave to bubble over a medium heat for 8–10 minutes to reduce by half.

About 5 minutes before the sweet potatoes have finished baking, grate the Cheddar over the top of them and sprinkle with Worcestershire sauce, if using.

Drain and rinse the beans. Stir through the tomato sauce and season (add a little Tabasco if you like). Heat until piping hot.

Chilli and sesame tuna topping

2 tablespoons sesame seeds
2 x 200g cans tuna in olive oil
1 fresh red/green chilli
2 spring onions (white bulbs and most
  of the green)
1 tablespoon finely chopped fresh coriander
2 tablespoons soy sauce
1 teaspoon toasted sesame oil
1 lime

Sprinkle the sesame seeds over the sweet potatoes while they are baking.

Drain and flake the tuna. Remove the seeds from the chilli, then finely chop. Thinly slice the spring onions on an angle. Combine these prepared ingredients in a bowl with the coriander, soy sauce and sesame oil. Zest the lime into the bowl and add the juice too. Mix everything well.

SWEET POTATO + SPINACH NIÇOISE SALAD

INGREDIENTS:	METHOD:

INGREDIENTS:

2 sweet potatoes
3 tablespoons olive oil, plus extra for drizzling
2 salmon fillets, 120–150g each
sea salt
lemon juice
2 eggs
10 cherry tomatoes
2 tablespoons wholegrain mustard
60g baby spinach leaves
30g pumpkin seeds

METHOD:

Preheat the oven to 180°C and boil a full kettle. Peel the sweet potatoes and cut into chunky, irregular-sized pieces. Place in a pan with a pinch of salt, cover with boiled water and simmer for 3 minutes.

Drain and place on a baking tray with a splash of oil and another pinch of salt. Bake for about 20 minutes until golden. Shake the tray every few minutes so the sweet potatoes don't catch.

While the sweet potatoes are in the oven, place the salmon on another baking tray, drizzle over a little oil, and season with a pinch of sea salt and a squeeze of lemon. Bake for 12 minutes.

Meanwhile, put the eggs in a pan, cover with boiled water and simmer for 9 minutes to hard-boil. Drain and place in a bowl of cold water to cool quickly, then peel and cut in half.

Cut the cherry tomatoes half. Whisk the mustard with the 3 tablespoons oil, a squeeze of lemon juice and salt to taste.

To pack: Allow the sweet potatoes and salmon to cool. Arrange the sweet potatoes, salmon (whole or flaked), eggs, tomato halves in the lunchboxes and top with the pumpkin seeds and spinach. Pack the mustard dressing separately.

TRY THIS…

· Replace the salmon with canned tuna. Drain and roughly flake the tuna, then mix with a dollop of Greek yoghurt, 1 tablespoon finely chopped fresh parsley, a squeeze of lemon juice and seasoning.

· Swap pumpkin seeds for mixed seeds or olives.

SWEET POTATO + RED LENTIL CAKES WITH A RAW SHREDDED SALAD

INGREDIENTS:

100g red lentils
2 sweet potatoes
2 teaspoons ground cumin
4 tablespoons snipped fresh chives
2 tablespoons sesame seeds
½ white cabbage
juice of 2 lemons
60g rocket

METHOD:

Preheat the oven to 200°C and boil a full kettle. Put the lentils in a pan with a pinch of salt, cover with boiled water and simmer over a medium heat for 10–12 minutes. Drain and rinse under cold water. Tip into a bowl.

While the lentils are cooking, peel the sweet potatoes and chop roughly into small pieces, then place in a pan with a pinch of salt. Cover with boiled water and simmer over a medium heat for 7–10 minutes until just soft. Drain and return to the pan. Using a potato masher, gently crush the potatoes. Add to the bowl with the lentils.

Season the mashed sweet potato and lentils with the cumin, half of the chives and a pinch of salt. Mix well. Shape into 6 cakes. Coat the top and bottom of each cake with sesame seeds and place on a lined baking tray. Bake for 10–12 minutes until golden. Flip over halfway through cooking.

Meanwhile, prepare the salad. Remove the outer leaves and stalk from the cabbage, then finely slice. Place in a bowl and toss with the lemon juice, remaining chives and a pinch of salt.

To pack: Allow the cakes to cool before packing. Place the cabbage salad on one side in the lunchboxes and the rocket on the other side. Arrange the cakes in the middle.

TRY THIS…

Add a heaped tablespoon of crumbled feta to the mashed sweet potato mix before forming it into cakes.

SWEET POTATO NACHOS

INGREDIENTS:	TRY THIS...

2 sweet potatoes
olive oil
2 tablespoons smoked paprika
1 red pepper
1 x 400g can kidney beans
1 x 400g can chickpeas
2 avocados
juice of ½ lemon
1 tablespoon finely chopped fresh coriander

METHOD:

Preheat the oven to 200°C. Scrub the sweet potatoes and pat dry, then slice into 1cm-thick rounds. Pile on a baking tray. Drizzle over a little oil and season with salt and the smoked paprika. Toss together until evenly coated, then spread out in one layer. Bake for 15–20 minutes until golden brown on both sides. Turn over midway through cooking. Cool.

While the sweet potatoes are baking, remove the core and seeds from the red pepper, then cut into strips. Drain and rinse the kidney beans and chickpeas. Place these prepared ingredients in a bowl and season.

Roughly chop the avocado flesh into 2cm dice and toss with the lemon juice and coriander. Season this guacamole.

To pack: Place the cooled sweet potato nachos on one side in the lunchboxes and the guacamole on the other side, with the bean salad in the middle.

· Turn this into Huevos Rancheros. Add cherry tomatoes, cut in half, and fry with the red pepper, beans and chickpeas in a splash of oil in an ovenproof frying pan for 10 minutes. Arrange the cooked sweet potato nachos over the surface and crack 2 eggs on top. Bake in a 180°C oven for 8–10 minutes until the eggs are cooked through. Serve warm with the guacamole or a dollop of crème fraîche.

· Pulled chicken is a great addition to the lunchboxes. Place 2 skinless boneless chicken breasts on a baking tray. Drizzle over a little oil and season with a pinch of sea salt. Bake in a 180°C oven for 15–18 minutes until cooked through. Cool slightly, then pull the chicken apart using two forks. Toast a tablespoon of smoked paprika or ground cumin in a dry pan for 2 minutes and stir through the pulled chicken with a little more oil, salt and pepper.

TIP: If you have leftover avocado, freeze it (without the stone). Add it frozen to a breakfast smoothie.

TUNA STEAK + SWEET POTATO NOODLES
WITH A SATAY SAUCE

INGREDIENTS:

2 large sweet potatoes
coconut/olive oil
200g sugarsnap peas
40g unsalted peanuts
2 fresh tuna steaks, 150–180g each
80g rocket
2 portions of Satay Dressing *(see page 156)*

METHOD:

Boil a full kettle. Peel the sweet potatoes and spiralise. Place in a pan with a splash of oil and cook over a medium-high heat, tossing gently with tongs, for 5–7 minutes until cooked through. Take care not to break up the noodles. Season and cool.

Place the sugarsnap peas in a bowl, cover with boiled water and leave for 3 minutes. Drain and rinse under cold water to stop the cooking.

While the sweet potatoes and sugarsnaps are being cooked, crush the peanuts and toast in a dry pan. Remove from the pan.

Turn the heat under the pan up to medium-high. Rub both sides of each tuna steak with oil and season with a pinch of sea salt. Place in the hot pan and sear for 1–2 minutes on each side. Remove from the pan and cool.

To pack: Pile the sweet potato noodles in one half of the lunchboxes. In the other half place the sugarsnap peas and rocket next to one another. Lay the cooked tuna steak on top of the noodles. When ready to serve, pour the dressing over all and sprinkle with the crushed, toasted peanuts.

TRY THIS...

Swap the tuna for salmon/peeled prawns. If using salmon fillets, add a splash of oil and pinch of salt, then bake in a 180°C oven for 12 minutes. For raw prawns, heat a pan with a splash of oil and cook the prawns for about 4 minutes until pink, stirring frequently.

SWEET POTATO MISO + CHORIZO HASH

INGREDIENTS:

3 sweet potatoes
80g chorizo
coconut/olive oil
100g green beans
80g chopped kale
100g Tenderstem broccoli
4 teaspoons miso paste
2 tablespoons honey
2 teaspoons ginger paste

METHOD:

Boil a full kettle. Scrub the sweet potatoes and chop into 3–4cm pieces. Place in a pan, cover with boiled water and add a pinch of salt. Cook for 3–4 minutes until just soft. Drain and set to one side.

Slice the chorizo into 1cm-thick rounds. Place the chorizo and cooked sweet potato in a frying pan with a splash of oil and fry for 2 minutes on each side until crisp. Remove and set aside (don't wash the pan).

Trim the green beans. Cut the green beans in half and the broccoli into shorter lengths if they are large. Place in a pan with the kale and broccoli. Cover with boiled water, add a pinch of salt and simmer over a medium heat for 4–5 minutes until just tender. Drain and rinse under cold water to stop the cooking.

Make the dressing by mixing together the miso, honey and ginger paste in the frying pan, adding a splash of hot water if needed to loosen (the dressing should be thick in consistency). Return the cooked sweet potato and chorizo to the pan and toss over a medium-low heat until the sauce thickens to a glaze and coats the sweet potato. Lightly crush the potato with the back of a fork.

To pack: Once cool, gently toss all the ingredients together, then spoon into the lunchboxes.

TRY THIS...

Scatter crumbled feta/sesame seeds/chilli over the hash in the lunchbox.

CARROT

CARROT, KALE + CHICKPEA SALAD WITH HONEY DRESSING + FETA

INGREDIENTS:

1 x 400g can chickpeas
coconut/olive oil
4 carrots
2 teaspoons cumin/fennel seeds
  (or ground is fine)
120g chopped kale
1 tablespoon finely chopped fresh parsley
80g feta

Dressing
1½ tablespoons honey
1 tablespoon olive oil
2 teaspoon cider vinegar

TRY THIS...

Stir some chopped unsalted pistachios, dried apricots, soaked couscous and torn fresh mint leaves through the carrot mix.

METHOD:

Preheat the oven to 200°C. Drain and rinse the chickpeas, then spread out on a baking tray. Mix with a little oil and seasoning. Roast for 10–15 minutes until crisp, shaking the baking tray every 5 minutes or so. Cool.

While the chickpeas are roasting, peel the carrots and cut into matchsticks. Set aside.

Toast the cumin/fennel seeds in a dry, medium-sized frying pan for about 3 minutes until fragrant. Smash into a powder with a pestle and mortar or the back of a rolling pin. Tip the spice powder back into the pan and add the carrots, kale and a little oil. Fry for 10–15 minutes until the carrots and kale are softening but still crunchy. Keep stirring as they fry.

Whisk together the dressing ingredients with a fork.

To pack: Toss the chickpeas and carrrot mix with the dressing, parsley and seasoning, then pack into the lunchboxes. Crumble the feta on top.

CARROT, PARMESAN, ROCKET, LENTIL + CHILLI SALAD

INGREDIENTS:

120g Puy lentils
6 carrots
olive oil
40g rocket
40g Parmesan shavings

Dressing
1 fresh red chilli
1 tablespoon honey
1 tablespoon cider vinegar
lemon juice

TRY THIS…

· Add a few pieces of crispy chorizo/bacon.

· Swap the honey for maple syrup.

· Add a finely sliced raw red onion.

METHOD:

Preheat the oven to 200°C and boil a full kettle. Put the lentils in a pan, cover with boiled water and add a pinch of salt. Cook for 15–20 minutes until al dente; drain.

Meanwhile, peel the carrots and cut into chunky matchsticks. Tip on to a baking tray. Mix through a little olive oil and seasoning. Roast for 25 minutes until golden brown, stirring every 5 minutes or so.

To make the dressing, finely chop the chilli, discarding the seeds. Combine in a bowl with the honey and vinegar. Add 2–3 tablespoons olive oil and lemon juice to taste. Season.

To pack: Mix the lentils with the carrots and spoon into lunchboxes. Top with the rocket and Parmesan. Pack the dressing separately.

PEPPERED MACKEREL + CARROT SALAD WITH HARISSA-YOGHURT DRESSING

INGREDIENTS:

2 peppered smoked mackerel fillets
6 carrots
2 handfuls of mixed dried fruit (any combination of raisins, sultanas, apricots and figs)
50g mixed salad leaves
40g toasted flaked almonds

Harissa dressing
2 teaspoons harissa paste
1 tablespoon Greek yoghurt
juice of ½ lemon
1 tablespoon olive oil

TRY THIS...

· Swap the harissa for horseradish cream/one of our pestos (*see pages 154–155*).

· Replace the mackerel with chicken breast strips fried in a little oil for 5 minutes.

· Add 2 chopped boiled sweet potatoes, peeled, cut into large chunks and boiled for 6 minutes.

METHOD:

Remove the skin from the mackerel and scoop out the brown centre with a teaspoon (this part is often bitter); discard any visible bones too. Chop or tear the mackerel into big pieces and set aside.

Peel and grate the carrots. Cut the dried fruit into small pieces.

Whisk together all the dressing ingredients with 2 tablespoons water.

To pack: Line the lunchboxes with the salad leaves and top with the carrots, mackerel, fruit and almonds. Pack the dressing separately.

CARROT + COURGETTE RIBBON SALAD WITH HONEY + ORANGE CHICKEN

INGREDIENTS:

2 skinless boneless chicken breasts
coconut/olive oil
1 tablespoon honey
2 oranges
60g crushed peanuts/flaked almonds/
    mixed seeds
5 carrots
2 courgettes

Dressing:
1 ½ tablespoons honey
2 tablespoons soy sauce
1 orange, juiced

METHOD:

Preheat the oven to 180°C. Place the chicken on a baking tray. Drizzle over a little oil and the honey. Zest the oranges directly on top. Season. Sprinkle the nuts alongside the chicken on the same tray. Bake for 15–18 minutes until the chicken is cooked through and the nuts are golden brown. Cool, then slice the chicken.

While the chicken is in the oven, remove the white part from two of the oranges and slice into 1cm-thick discs. Peel the carrots and slice into ribbons with a peeler. Repeat with the courgettes but discarding the watery centre.

Whisk together the ingredients for the dressing with the juice from the third orange.

To pack: Spread the vegetable ribbons in the lunchboxes. Add a layer of orange slices and top with the sliced chicken and nuts. Pack the dressing separately.

TRY THIS...

· Swap the courgettes or carrots for ribbons of ready-cooked and peeled beetroot.

· Add 100g quinoa, simmered for 8–10 minutes, and a handful of chopped fresh herbs.

CHICKEN CARROT COCONUT SALAD

INGREDIENTS:	METHOD:
2 skinless boneless chicken breasts 3 tablespoons desiccated coconut coconut/olive oil 5 carrots 60g rocket 2 handfuls of pomegranate seeds 2 portions of Coconut-lime Dressing *(see page 153)*	Preheat the oven to 180°C. Place the chicken on a baking tray. Sprinkle over the desiccated coconut and add a splash of oil and a pinch of salt. Bake for 15–18 minutes until cooked through. Cool, then slice at an angle. While the chicken is cooking, peel the carrots and spiralise (or slice into strips with a peeler). *To pack:* Place the spiralised carrots in one half of the lunchboxes and the rocket in the other half. Fan the sliced chicken across the rocket and carrot. Sprinkle over the pomegranate seeds. Pack the dressing separately.

TRY THIS...

Swap the chicken for cooked peeled prawns.

CARROT NOODLES + PEANUT TERIYAKI SALMON

INGREDIENTS:	METHOD:
2 skinless salmon fillets, about 150g each 2 tablespoons roughly chopped fresh coriander olive oil 2 tablespoons sesame seeds 4 carrots 2 courgettes 2 portions of Peanut Teriyaki Sauce *(see page 156)*	Preheat the oven to 180°C. Place the salmon on a baking tray. Mix together the coriander, a splash of olive oil and the sesame seeds. Spread over the salmon. Bake for 12 minutes. Cool. Meanwhile, peel the carrots and spiralise. Trim the courgettes and spiralise. Place both in a bowl and toss together. *To pack:* Place the carrot and courgette noodles in the lunchboxes and lay the salmon fillets across them. Pack the Peanut Teriyaki Sauce separately.

CARROT RIBBON, CHICKEN + POMEGRANATE QUINOA TABBOULEH

INGREDIENTS:

100g quinoa
2 skinless boneless chicken breasts
olive oil
6 spring onions (white bulbs and most of green)
10 cherry tomatoes
4 carrots
2 tablespoons finely chopped fresh mixed herbs
   (parsley, mint, chives)
2 handfuls of pomegranate seeds
lemon juice

TRY THIS...

Add roasted sweet potato cubes, crumbled feta and dried chilli flakes instead of (or as well as) chicken and pomegranate.

METHOD:

Boil a full kettle. Put the quinoa in a pan, cover with boiled water and add a pinch of salt. Cook for 8–10 minutes until al dente. Drain and rinse with cold water.

While the quinoa is cooking, finely slice the chicken and place in a frying pan with a little oil and seasoning. Finely slice the spring onions and add to the pan. Fry over a medium heat for 5 minutes until the chicken is cooked through, stirring frequently.

Combine the quinoa, chicken and spring onions in a bowl. Cool.

Halve the cherry tomatoes. Peel the carrots and slice into ribbons with a peeler. Add the tomatoes and carrots to the bowl, then mix through the herbs and pomegranate seeds. Season to taste with salt, pepper, lemon juice and olive oil.

To pack: Spoon into two lunchboxes.

CHOPPED SOBA MISO SALAD

INGREDIENTS:

METHOD:

Boil a full kettle. Put the noodles in a pan, cover with boiled water and add a pinch of salt. Cook for 5–8 minutes until al dente. Drain and rinse in cold water to cool quickly, then roughly chop up using kitchen scissors.

While the noodles are cooking, put the edamame in a bowl of cold water and set aside to thaw for 5 minutes; drain. Peel the carrots and spiralise. Remove the tough outer leaves and core from the red cabbage, then thinly slice. Thinly slice the spring onions at an angle. Toast the sesame seeds in a small pan until golden.

Put the miso in a bowl. Zest the limes into the bowl and squeeze in the juice. Add a splash of hot water and mix well.

To pack: Arrange the vegetables and noodles in the lunchboxes (or mix them together) and sprinkle the toasted sesame seeds on top. Pack the dressing separately.

100g soba noodles
100g frozen shelled edamame beans
4 carrots
¼ red cabbage
2 spring onions (white bulbs and most
    of the green part)
2 tablespoons sesame seeds
4 teaspoons miso paste
2 limes

HERB + NUT-STUFFED TOMATOES

INGREDIENTS:

150g quinoa
6 medium beef tomatoes
2 garlic cloves
coconut/olive oil
200g baby spinach leaves
2 tablespoons each roughly chopped
    fresh parsley and mint
1 lemon
100g chopped mixed nuts (e.g. hazelnuts,
    unsalted cashew and walnuts)
50g grated mozzarella

TRY THIS...

· Add 2 handfuls of pulled chicken *(see page 30)*
  or diced cooked sausages to the quinoa.

· Experiment with different herbs such as chervil
  and chives.

METHOD:

Preheat the oven to 180°C and boil a full kettle.
Put the quinoa in a pan, cover with boiled water
and add a pinch of salt. Cook for 8–10 minutes
until al dente. Drain.

While the quinoa is cooking, slice the top off
each tomato and scoop out the seeds and fleshy
part (don't throw this away). Carefully slice a
very thin layer off the bottom of each tomato to
make sure it will sit upright. Place the tomatoes
on a baking tray lined with a sheet of baking
parchment. Set aside.

Peel and finely dice the garlic. Place in a pan
with a splash of oil and cook over a medium
heat for 2 minutes. Add the tomato seeds/flesh,
150g of the baby spinach and the herbs. Cook
for 5 minutes, stirring constantly.

Add the cooked quinoa to the pan, season and
stir well. Cook for a further 3–5 minutes. Zest the
lemon into the pan and add the juice too, with a
splash of water if the mix starts to catch.

Toast the mixed nuts in a dry pan until golden
brown. Chop the nuts, then mix half into the
quinoa. Divide the quinoa mix among the
tomatoes. Cover the baking tray with foil and
bake for 15 minutes.

Top the tomatoes with the grated mozzarella and
remaining chopped nuts, then bake for a further
5 minutes.

To pack: Allow the tomatoes to cool, then place
carefully, side by side, in the lunchboxes and pile
the remaining spinach leaves on top.

TOM YUM SOUP

INGREDIENTS:

1 small white onion
2–3 fresh red birds' eye chillies (optional)
coconut/olive oil
rice wine vinegar (optional)
a flavour bundle: 2 lemongrass stalks, 4 kaffir
    lime leaves (or 2 chopped limes) and 20g piece
    galangal root (or fresh ginger), peeled and
    roughly chopped, all wrapped together in
    muslin or a J-cloth and tied with a length of
    string so it is easy to remove later
1 x 200ml can coconut milk
8 medium tomatoes
2 red peppers
2 courgettes
lime juice
soy sauce
chopped fresh coriander

METHOD:

Boil a full kettle.

Peel and finely dice the onion (and chillies, if using). Place in a pan with a splash of oil and cook over a medium heat for 3 minutes. Add a splash of rice wine vinegar (if using) and cook for a further minute. Add the flavour bundle, coconut milk and 250ml boiled water and cook for a further 5 minutes.

Meanwhile, dice the tomatoes into 1cm cubes. Remove the core and seeds from the peppers, then cut, along with the courgettes, into cubes similar in size to the tomatoes. Add all these vegetables to the pan and continue to cook for 8 minutes over a medium heat. Stir occasionally.

Remove from the heat. Discard the flavour bundle. Season the soup with lime juice, soy sauce and chopped coriander to taste.

To pack: Cool, then pour into watertight containers, to prevent leakage.

TRY THIS...

· Add raw peeled prawns for the final few minutes of cooking and simmer until they turn pink.

· Bulk this up with more vegetables. Broccoli works really well – add to the pan at the same time as the tomatoes, courgettes and red peppers.

SAMBOL RYE

INGREDIENTS:

1 red onion
coconut/olive oil
2 teaspoons ground ginger
2 teaspoons chilli powder
4 tablespoons desiccated coconut
2 beef tomatoes
1 handful of cherry tomatoes
2 slices rye bread
80g rocket/baby spinach leaves
2 lemon wedges (optional)

METHOD:

Peel and finely dice the red onion. Place in a pan with a splash of oil and cook over a medium heat for 3–4 minutes. Stir in the ground ginger and chilli powder and cook for a further 2 minutes. Remove from the heat.

In another pan toast the desiccated coconut over a medium heat until golden. Add half of the coconut to the onions.

Roughly dice the beef tomatoes and add to the onions. Return to the heat and cook for 3–4 minutes until the tomatoes start to break down. Season and cool.

Slice the cherry tomatoes in half.

To pack: Place the rye bread on the bottom of the lunchboxes. Top with a layer of half the rocket/spinach, followed by the onion and tomato mixture (this arrangement prevents the rye from going soggy.) Scatter the halved cherry tomatoes and the remaining toasted coconut and rocket/spinach over the top. Tuck a wedge of lemon into each lunchbox, if using.

HARISSA, TOMATO + MOZZARELLA SALAD

INGREDIENTS:

250g cherry tomatoes (a mixture of colours
  works well)
1 handful of fresh basil leaves
1 handful of fresh parsley
1 cucumber
15–20 small mozzarella pearls

Harissa dressing
2–3 teaspoons harissa paste
juice of ½ lemon
2 tablespoons olive oil
2 teaspoons honey or sugar

TRY THIS…

· Replace the harissa with one of our pestos
  (see pages 154–155) or tahini.

· Add an avocado, diced, or a few slices of
  Parma ham, torn into pieces.

METHOD:

Mix all the ingredients for the dressing together
with 1 tablespoon water and season.

Slice the tomatoes in half and place in a bowl.
Tear over the basil. Finely chop the parsley and
sprinkle on top.

Slice the cucumber in half lengthways and scoop
out the seeds with a teaspoon. Cut across into
chunks on an angle. Add to the bowl along with
the mozzarella. Mix everything together.

To pack: Spoon the salad into the lunchboxes.
Pack the dressing separately.

RIBOLATA SALAD

INGREDIENTS:

160g chopped kale
2 carrots
1 courgette
1 leek
olive oil
1 teaspoon dried chilli flakes
1 x 400g can cannellini beans
4 tablespoons chopped mixed fresh herbs
2 handfuls of mixed cherry tomatoes

METHOD:

Boil a full kettle. Place the kale in a bowl, cover with boiled water and leave for 5 minutes. Drain and rinse under cold water.

While the kale is blanching, peel the carrots and slice into 5mm-thick rounds. Slice the courgette into 5mm-thick rounds. Slice the leek into 1cm-thick rounds.

Put the leek in a frying pan with a glug of olive oil, a pinch of salt and the chilli flakes and cook over a medium heat, stirring frequently, for 5 minutes until soft. Tip into a bowl and add the carrots and courgette. Season.

Add the kale, drained and rinsed beans, herbs and sliced cherry tomatoes. Toss together gently.

To pack: Spoon into the lunchboxes.

TRY THIS...

· Add 2 handfuls of pulled chicken *(see page 30)*.

· Top with a dollop of Green Pesto *(see page 154)*.

TIP: Ribolata is a hearty Tuscan soup that is great for using up leftovers. We have turned the common ingredients into a salad here.

TOMATO, SAUSAGE + BUTTER BEAN SALAD

4 pork or beef sausages
olive oil
1 tablespoon smoked paprika
1 teaspoon dried chilli flakes
1 x 400g can butter beans
2 tablespoons chopped fresh mixed herbs (basil
   and parsley work well)
2 red peppers
10 cherry tomatoes
2 tablespoons balsamic vinegar (optional)

Using scissors, cut the sausages into 4cm discs.
Place in a pan with a splash of oil, the smoked
paprika and chilli flakes and fry over a medium-
low heat for 10–15 minutes until browned all
over and cooked through. Cool.

While the sausages are cooking, drain and rinse
the butter beans. Toss them with the fresh herbs
and season with a pinch of salt.

Remove the core and seeds from the red peppers,
then cut into chunky pieces. Halve the cherry
tomatoes. Mix the peppers and tomatoes with
the sausage and drizzle with balsamic vinegar.

To pack: Spoon the sausage mix into one side of
each lunchbox alongside the herby butter beans.

TRY THIS… Replace the sausages with half the
amount of chorizo – omit the paprika and chilli,
and cook for 5–8 minutes.

CANDIED MISO TOMATO SALAD

6 streaky bacon rashers
150g chopped kale
40g pecans
2 tablespoons honey, plus extra for drizzling
4 teaspoons miso paste
2 teaspoons ginger paste
3 handfuls of cherry tomatoes

Preheat the oven to 200°C and boil a full kettle.
Lay the bacon rashers on a baking tray and bake
for 5–8 minutes until crisp.

Meanwhile, place the kale in a bowl and cover
with boiled water. Leave for 5 minutes, then
drain and rinse under cold water. Set to one side.

While the bacon and kale are baking/blanching,
place the pecans in a frying pan and lightly toast
over a medium heat for 2 minutes until golden.
Add a drizzle of honey and briefly toss the nuts
until caramelised. Pour on to a sheet of baking
parchment and leave to cool before chopping
roughly.

To make the miso dressing, put the miso,
2 tablespoons honey and the ginger paste in a
pan with a splash of water (not too much as the
dressing should be thick in consistency). Cook
over a medium heat for 1–2 minutes until just
thickening. Cool.

Slice the cherry tomatoes in half.

To pack: Line the bottom of the lunchboxes with
the kale. Scatter the cherry tomatoes and pecans
over the kale. Roughly break up the bacon on
top. Pack the dressing separately.

RED
PEPPER

ONE-PAN LEMON CHICKEN + CHORIZO

3 peppers (mixed colours)
olive oil
½ lemon
2 skinless boneless chicken breasts
80g chorizo
4 spring onions (white bulbs only)
1 fresh red chilli
40g toasted flaked almonds
50g baby spinach leaves

Remove the core and seeds from the peppers, then cut into roughly 3cm chunks. Place in a medium-sized with a little olive oil and fry over a low heat for 10–15 minutes until soft. Keep stirring regularly.

About 5 minutes after you start frying the peppers, cut the lemon half into chunks and squeeze the juice into the pan. Add the squeezed chunks to the pan too.

Slice the chicken breasts into thin strips and the chorizo into discs. Once the peppers have been cooking for 10 minutes, add the chicken and chorizo to the pan and cook for a further 5–10 minutes over a medium heat until the chicken is cooked through, stirring frequently. Discard the lemon chunks.

Finely slice the spring onions. Finely slice the chilli, discarding the seeds. Stir both of these through the pepper mix. Season.

To pack: Once the chicken and pepper salad is cool, spoon into the lunchboxes. Sprinkle with the flaked almonds and pile the spinach on top.

TRY THIS… Add a 400g can of butter beans or kidney beans, drained and rinsed.

PEANUT-DRESSED CHICKEN, BEANSPROUT + RED PEPPER SALAD

180g Tenderstem broccoli
3 red peppers
coconut/olive oil
2 skinless boneless chicken breasts
200g beansprouts
2 tablespoons finely chopped fresh coriander
3–4 tablespoons peanut butter (preferably crunchy and sugar-free)
2 tablespoons soy sauce
1 lime

Boil a full kettle. Trim the ends off the broccoli, then cut each stem in half at an angle and place in a pan. Cover with boiled water and add a pinch of salt. Cook for 3–4 minutes until al dente. Drain and rinse under cold water.

Remove the core and seeds from the red peppers, then cut into strips. Fry with a splash of oil for 15 minutes until very soft.

Meanwhile, slice the chicken into thin strips. Add to the peppers 10 minutes after the start of cooking. Keep stirring. Add the beansprouts for the final minute of cooking. Turn into a bowl and mix in the broccoli and coriander.

Put the peanut butter in a small pan and allow to melt over a low heat. Remove from the heat. Whisk through the soy sauce. Zest the lime into the pan and add the juice too. Taste and add more soy sauce if needed plus a splash of hot water if the dressing seems too thick.

To pack: Spoon the salad into the lunchboxes. Pack the dressing separately.

TRY THIS… Serve with Coconut-lime Dressing *(see page 153)* instead.

OREGANO-BAKED FETA WITH A MEDITERRANEAN SALAD

INGREDIENTS:

120g feta (or halloumi/tofu)
1 tablespoon chopped fresh oregano
   (or 2 teaspoons dried Italian herbs/
   oregano/thyme)
olive oil
4 jarred roasted red peppers (or 3 raw red
   peppers, cut into matchsticks)
2 handfuls of cherry tomatoes
1 garlic clove
1 x 400g can butter beans/kidney beans
2 teaspoons red wine vinegar
2 tablespoons finely chopped fresh parsley

TRY THIS…

· Toast some rye bread and chop into croutons.
  Pack separately to garnish the salad.

· Add 2 sweet potatoes, peeled, cut into 2cm
  chunks and boiled for 6–8 minutes.

· Stir 80g cooked wild rice into the bean and
  pepper salad.

· Pile a handful of baby spinach leaves on top
  of the feta in the lunchboxes.

METHOD:

Preheat the oven to 200°C. Line a baking sheet with a piece of foil (large enough to wrap up the feta). Cut the feta into roughly 2cm pieces and place on the foil with the oregano, some salt and pepper and a little olive oil. Mix well, then wrap up like a parcel. Bake for 10 minutes.

Meanwhile, cut the peppers into strips and halve the cherry tomatoes. Place these in a bowl. Peel the garlic and crush on top. Add the drained and rinsed beans, a little olive oil, the vinegar and parsley and mix thoroughly. Season.

To pack: Spoon the bean and pepper salad into the lunchboxes. When the feta has cooled, arrange it on top of the salad.

RED PEPPER + AUBERGINE PASTA
WITH RED PESTO

INGREDIENTS:

200g wholemeal fusilli
coconut/olive oil
1 large aubergine
2 portions of Red Pepper Pesto *(see page 155)*
3 jarred roasted red peppers
lemon juice (optional)
40g toasted pine nuts
grated Parmesan/crumbled feta, to garnish
40g rocket

TRY THIS…

· Fry 150g lean beef mince until well browned.
  Stir through the pasta salad before packing in
  the lunchboxes.

· Bake 2 cod fillets, each topped with a teaspoon
  of Red Pepper Pesto, in a 180°C oven for
  12 minutes. Place the cooled fish on the
  pasta salad and finish with the nuts, cheese
  and rocket.

· Turn this into a hot gratin to eat at home:
  sprinkle equal amounts of grated Parmesan
  and breadcrumbs on top of the pasta salad
  in a baking dish and bake in a 200°C oven
  for 10–15 minutes.

METHOD:

Boil a full kettle. Put the pasta in a pan with a
pinch of salt and cover with boiled water. Cook
for 12–14 minutes until al dente. Drain and toss
with a little oil to prevent sticking.

While the pasta is cooking, remove the stalk from
the aubergine, then cut into 2cm chunks. Place in
a pan, cover with boiled water and add a pinch of
salt. Boil for 2 minutes until the aubergine is just
starting to soften. Drain and rinse under cold water.

Tip the aubergine into a frying pan and add a
little oil. Fry over a high heat for 4 minutes until
cooked through and slightly crisp. Keep stirring.
Remove from the heat and mix through the pasta
with the pesto.

Finely slice the red peppers and add to the pan.
Season and add a little extra oil or some lemon
juice if needed.

To pack: Spoon the pasta salad into the lunchboxes.
Scatter the pine nuts and cheese on the salad and
top with the rocket.

RED PEPPER + FENNEL QUINOA SALAD WITH CHORIZO

INGREDIENTS:

120g quinoa
1 fennel bulb
2 red peppers
1 garlic clove
coconut/olive oil
80g chorizo
2 teaspoons cumin seeds
1 tablespoon honey
lemon juice

TRY THIS...

· Swap the quinoa for a 400g can of butter beans, drained and rinsed.

· Instead of frying the fennel, use it raw.

METHOD:

Boil a full kettle. Put the quinoa in a pan, cover with boiled water and add a pinch of salt. Cook for 8–10 minutes until al dente. Drain and set aside.

While the quinoa is cooking, remove the outer leaves and core from the fennel, then finely slice. Remove the core and seeds from the red peppers, then finely slice. Peel and crush the garlic. Place the fennel, red peppers and garlic in a frying pan with a little oil and fry over a low heat for 10 minutes until soft. Keep stirring.

Turn up the heat and fry for a further 5 minutes until slightly crisp. Stir the pepper mix through the quinoa and set aside.

Slice or dice the chorizo, then fry with the cumin seeds in the frying pan for 2 minutes until crisp.

Mix the honey and a little lemon juice through the quinoa salad. Season.

To pack: Once cool, spoon the quinoa salad into the lunchboxes and scatter the chorizo on top.

TIP: Keep the fine fennel leaves and scatter over the chorizo for extra aniseed flavour.

STUFFED PEPPERS WITH TOMATOES, COUSCOUS, + KALE + WALNUT PESTO

3 red peppers
olive oil
100g couscous
150g chopped kale
2 handfuls of cherry tomatoes
60g walnuts
2 portions of Kale and Walnut Pesto *(see page 155)*
lemon juice (optional)

Preheat the oven to 200°C and boil a full kettle. Cut the peppers in half vertically and scoop out the seeds and white ribs. Place the halves skin side down on a baking tray and drizzle over a little oil. Season. Bake for 25 minutes until soft.

While the peppers are in the oven, put the couscous in a bowl and cover with boiled water (the water level should be about 5mm above the couscous). Cover with clingfilm and set aside for at least 5 minutes.

Meanwhile, place the chopped kale in a bowl, cover with boiled water and leave for 5 minutes. Drain and rinse under cold water.

Halve the cherry tomatoes. Lightly crush the walnuts, then toast in a dry pan until golden.

Fluff up the couscous with a fork. Mix together the couscous, kale, tomatoes, walnuts and most of the pesto. Season and add lemon juice and/or olive oil to taste. Spoon into the pepper halves.

To pack: Cool the peppers before placing 3 halves in each lunchbox, in one layer. Top each with a little extra pesto.

TRY THIS… Switch the couscous to quinoa.

SPINACH + PEA-STUFFED PEPPERS WITH GOATS' CHEESE

3 red peppers
olive oil
2 red onions
200g frozen peas
200g baby spinach leaves
15 fresh basil leaves
1 x 400g can chickpeas
lemon juice
100g goats' cheese

Preheat the oven to 210°C. Slice the peppers in half vertically and scoop out the seeds and white ribs. Place the halves skin side down on a baking tray. Drizzle over a little oil and season, then bake for 20 minutes until soft.

Meanwhile, peel and finely slice the onions. Place in a frying pan with a splash of oil and cook over a low heat for 10 minutes until completely soft. Thaw the peas in a bowl of cold water for 1–2 minutes; drain.

Add the spinach to the pan and fry for 2 minutes until wilted. Remove from the heat and stir through the peas, torn basil and drained and rinsed chickpeas. Season well, adding lemon juice and more olive oil to taste.

When the peppers are nearly ready, remove from the oven and fill generously with the spinach mixture (if you have extra you can serve it on the side). Sprinkle over the goats' cheese. Place back in the oven and bake for a final 5 minutes until the cheese melts and turns slightly golden.

To pack: Cool the pepper halves before placing in the lunchboxes, in one layer.

RED PEPPER + BUTTER BEAN HUMMUS WITH ROASTED SQUASH + PARMESAN

INGREDIENTS:

1 small butternut squash
coconut/olive oil
1 fresh red chilli
2 jarred roasted red peppers
40g mixed salad leaves
40g Parmesan shavings
½ lemon
2 portions of Red Pepper and
    Butter Bean Hummus *(see page 157)*

TRY THIS...

· Add 1–2 teaspoons harissa paste to the hummus.

· Swap the jarred peppers for 2 raw red peppers, cut into strips and roasted with the squash.

METHOD:

Preheat the oven to 200°C and boil a full kettle. Peel the squash and cut into chunks or sticks about 5mm thick, discarding the seeds. Place in a pan, cover with boiled water and add a pinch of salt. Boil for 3 minutes.

Drain the squash and place on a baking tray. Drizzle over a little oil and season. Roast for 20 minutes, flipping the pieces over halfway through cooking. Cool.

While the squash is roasting, finely dice the chilli, discarding the seeds. Slice the red peppers into strips.

To pack: Mix the salad leaves with the Parmesan shavings and chilli and pile on one side of the lunchboxes. Pile the peppers and squash on the other side. Tuck a wedge of lemon into each box. Pack the hummus separately.

PADRON PEPPER, CHORIZO + HALLOUMI SALAD

INGREDIENTS:

120g quinoa (black works well here)

1 lime

2 spring onions (white bulbs and most of the green)

60g rocket

2 tablespoons chopped fresh coriander

coconut/olive oil

a mixture of peppers such as 5 padron peppers
    and 5 small sweet peppers

sea salt

80g chorizo

140g halloumi

TRY THIS…

If you can't find padron or small sweet peppers, you can use 5 regular peppers, each cut into 4 big wedges or 'boats'. Fry, then fill them with the quinoa mix.

METHOD:

Boil a full kettle. Put the quinoa in a pan, cover with boiled water and add a pinch of salt. Cook for 8–10 minutes until al dente. Drain and rinse with cold water to cool, then zest in the lime and add the juice too. Mix through the spring onions and coriander.

While the quinoa is cooking, heat a frying pan with a splash of oil, add the whole peppers and fry over a medium heat until they have browned and blistered. Tip into a bowl and season with sea salt. Set aside.

Slice the chorizo into 2cm-thick rounds and the halloumi into 1cm chunks. Heat another frying pan with a splash of oil and cook the chorizo and halloumi for 2 minutes on each side until golden.

To pack: Spoon the quinoa salad into the lunchboxes and top with the peppers, chorizo and halloumi. Scatter rocket over the top of the salad.

BEETROOT

BEETROOT CORONATION CHICKEN

INGREDIENTS:

2 skinless boneless chicken breasts
1 tablespoon coconut oil
2 tablespoons curry powder
2 teaspoons tomato purée
8 ready-cooked and peeled beetroots
1 cucumber
1 lemon
4 tablespoons Greek yoghurt
about 2 tablespoons honey, to taste
80g toasted flaked almonds

TRY THIS...

· Garnish with a small handful of chopped
  fresh coriander or chopped dried apricots/
  cranberries.

· Serve for dinner with a roasted sweet potato
  jacket and spinach leaves.

METHOD:

Preheat the oven to 180°C. Line a baking
tray then place the chicken breasts on the tray,
rub them with coconut oil, curry powder, the
tomato paste and a pinch of salt. Bake in the
oven for 15–18 minutes. Allow to cool then
slice at an angle.

While the chicken is cooling, cut the beetroots
into 1cm cubes. Slice the cucumber in half
lengthways and scoop out the seeds with a metal
spoon. Slice the halves in half lengthways, then
finely dice.

Put the beetroot and cucumber in a bowl. Zest
and juice the lemon and add with the yoghurt
and a little honey. Mix and season. Add further
honey to taste.

To pack: Spoon the salad into one side of the
lunchboxes and the chicken into the other (or
gently fold the chicken through the salad first).
Sprinkle the almonds on top.

BALSAMIC, BEETROOT + RED ONION SALAD WITH GOATS' CHEESE

INGREDIENTS:

2 red onions
6–8 ready-cooked and peeled beetroots
1 x 400g can chickpeas
80g mixed nuts
2 tablespoons honey
2 tablespoons balsamic vinegar
30g rocket
60g soft goats' cheese

TRY THIS...

· Add some picked and chopped fresh rosemary/
  thyme to the vegetables while they roast.

· Swap the chickpeas for cooked pasta
  (preferably conchiglie).

METHOD:

Preheat the oven to 200°C. Peel the onions, then chop with the beetroots into roughly 2cm cubes. Pile on a baking tray with the drained and rinsed chickpeas, roughly crushed nuts, honey and balsamic. Toss together, then spread out.

Roast for 10 minutes until everything is slightly crisp in parts. Shake the tray every few minutes to move the ingredients.

To pack: Allow to cool, then season. Pack the salad in the lunchboxes and top with the rocket leaves. Scatter lumps of goats' cheese on top of the rocket.

HERBY QUINOA SALAD WITH SMOKED SALMON, PEAS + BEETROOT

INGREDIENTS:

120g quinoa (or bulghur wheat)
6–8 ready-cooked and peeled beetroots
4 slices smoked salmon
40g pumpkin seeds
200g frozen peas
4 tablespoons finely chopped mixed fresh herbs
    (parsley, chives, dill, mint and/or chervil)
juice of ½ lemon
olive oil

TRY THIS…

· Stir through a tablespoon of one of our pestos (*see pages 154–155*) with the oil at the end.

· Add a handful each of blueberries and unsalted cashew nuts instead of smoked salmon.

· Swap the smoked salmon for a baked trout fillet. Place the trout on a baking tray, sprinkle with a splash of oil and pinch of salt, and bake in a 180°C oven for 12 minutes. Cool, then flake on top of the salad in the lunchboxes.

METHOD:

Boil a full kettle. Put the quinoa in a pan and cover generously with boiled water. Add salt and cook for 8–10 minutes until al dente. Drain.

While the quinoa is cooking, cut the beetroot into 1cm cubes. Slice the salmon into strips. Toast the pumpkin seeds in a dry pan for 2 minutes until they start to pop.

Thaw the peas in a bowl of cold water for 1–2 minutes; drain. Mix the peas, herbs and lemon juice through the quinoa.

To pack: When the quinoa is cool, fold through the beetroot, salmon and pumpkin seeds, then add a splash of olive oil and season to taste. Divide between the lunchboxes.

TIP: Keep herbs fresh for longer in the fridge by covering loosely with a slightly damp tea towel or kitchen paper.

ORANGE + BEETROOT SALAD WITH ORANGE DRESSING

INGREDIENTS:

120g Puy lentils
6–8 ready-cooked and peeled beetroots
4 oranges
40g flaked almonds
50g walnuts
50g rocket

Orange shallot dressing
2 shallots/1 small white onion
1 tablespoon olive oil
1 tablespoon honey
juice of 2 oranges
1 tablespoon red wine vinegar/cider vinegar

TRY THIS…

· Top with some crumbled goats' cheese and
  a ready-made balsamic glaze.

· Add salmon: place a 150g salmon fillet in a
  small baking dish and top with a tablespoon
  of honey or maple syrup and some orange zest,
  then bake in a 180°C oven for 12 minutes.
  Cool before placing on the salad (whole or
  flaked) and topping with rocket.

METHOD:

Preheat the oven to 200°C and boil a full kettle.
Put the lentils in a pan, cover with boiled water
and add a pinch of salt. Cook for 15–20 minutes
until al dente. Drain.

While the lentils are cooking, slice the beetroots
into 1cm-thick discs. Repeat with the oranges,
picking out any seeds. Pull off the orange peel
and add to the lentils while they cook, for
extra flavour.

To make the dressing, peel and finely chop the
onion. Tip into a small pan and fry over a low
heat in the tablespoon of oil for 10 minutes until
softened. Add the rest of the dressing ingredients
and reduce over a low heat until just thickened and
slightly syrupy (check by seeing how the dressing
runs off a spoon).

Toast the nuts in a dry pan until golden brown.

To pack: Mix all the prepared ingredients and
dressing together and cool, then pack in the
lunchboxes. Top with the rocket leaves.

TIP: Make a bigger batch of the dressing – it will keep for 5 days in the fridge.

WILD RICE + BEETROOT KEDGEREE

INGREDIENTS:

180g mixed wild and brown rice
2 eggs
1 garlic clove
2cm piece fresh ginger
2 spring onions (white bulbs only)
coconut/olive oil
2 teaspoons curry powder
80g frozen shelled edamame beans
6 ready-cooked and peeled beetroots
50g baby spinach leaves
4 tablespoons Greek yoghurt (optional)
juice of 1 lemon

METHOD:

Preheat the oven to 200°C and boil a full kettle.
Put the rice in a pan with a pinch of salt. Cover
with boiled water and simmer over a medium
heat for 15–20 minutes until al dente. Drain and
rinse under cold water.

While the rice is cooking, put the eggs in
another pan, cover with boiled water and boil
for 9 minutes. Rinse under cold water, then peel
and cut in half.

Peel the garlic and crush into a frying pan. Peel
the ginger and grate into the pan. Finely chop
the spring onions and add to the pan along with
a little oil. Fry over a medium heat for 2 minutes,
stirring. Stir in the curry powder and fry for
another 2 minutes. Remove from the heat.

Thaw the edamame in a bowl of cold water for
1–2 minutes; drain.

Finely chop the beetroots and stir through the
spice base along with the rice, spinach, edamame
and yoghurt. Add lemon juice to taste and season.

To pack: Once the kedgeree is cool, pack into the
lunchboxes and set the egg halves on top.

TRY THIS...

Add salmon. Dress 2 x 150g salmon fillets
with a little grating of fresh ginger, a sprinkle
of turmeric and salt and a drizzle of olive oil,
then bake in a 180°C oven for 12 minutes.
Cool. Flake and fold through the salad.

BEETROOT HUMMUS WITH WILD RICE + KALE

INGREDIENTS:

180g mixed wild and long-grain rice
150g chopped kale
10 breakfast radishes
1 cucumber
10 fresh mint leaves
1 lemon
2 portions of Beetroot Hummus *(see page 157)*
2 tablespoons mixed seeds (optional)

TRY THIS...

Add smoked or baked salmon. Place a 150g salmon fillet on a baking tray and bake in a 180°C oven for 12 minutes. Cool, then flake over.

METHOD:

Boil a full kettle. Put the rice in a pan, cover with boiled water and add a pinch of salt. Simmer over a medium-high heat for 10–12 minutes until al dente. Drain and rinse under cold water. Tip into a bowl.

While the rice is cooking, put the chopped kale in a bowl, cover with boiled water and leave for 5 minutes. Drain and rinse under cold water. Remove the stalks from the radishes, then slice in half lengthways. Cut the cucumber in half lengthways and scoop out the seeds with a teaspoon. Slice each half across into shards.

Roughly chop the mint and add to the rice. Zest and juice the lemon and add to the rice. Season and toss together with a little olive oil.

To pack: Put the rice in one half of the lunchboxes. Place the kale in the other half. On top of the kale, arrange the radishes on one half and the cucumber on the other. Dollop the hummus in one corner of the rice. Sprinkle the rice with the mixed seeds.

SPIRALISED BEETROOT VEGETABLE RAGU

INGREDIENTS:

100g green beans
6–8 ready-cooked and peeled beetroots
150g chopped kale
½ red onion
20 cherry tomatoes
1 courgette
2 tablespoons balsamic vinegar
coconut/olive oil
20 fresh basil leaves

TRY THIS…

· Any spiralised vegetable will work – spiralised butternut squash, for example.

· Finish with a sprinkling of feta.

METHOD:

Preheat the oven to 190°C and boil a full kettle.

Trim the green beans. Place in a bowl with the kale and cover with boiled water. Leave for 5 minutes, then drain.

Meanwhile, spiralise the beetroots. Place on a baking tray. Add the drained beans and kale.

Peel and roughly chop the onion. Add to the baking tray. Cut the cherry tomatoes in half. Slice the courgette into medium-sized rounds. Add both to the baking tray.

Sprinkle over the balsamic vinegar, a splash of oil and a pinch of salt and toss everything together. Spread out, then roast for 10–12 minutes until just cooked through.

To pack: Cool before packing in the lunchboxes. Scatter the torn basil leaves on top.

GOATS' CHEESE RYE WITH BEETROOT HUMMUS

INGREDIENTS:

1 lemon
60g soft goats' cheese
20 fresh chives
2 slices rye bread
2 portions of Beetroot Hummus *(see page 157)*
50g rocket
50g mixed seeds

TRY THIS...

Pack some smoked salmon too, and pile onto the goats' cheese toasts before eating.

METHOD:

Zest the lemon into a bowl and add the goats' cheese. Finely chop the chives and add. Mix well.

Toast the rye bread. Cut each slice into quarters.

To pack: Wrap/pack all the elements separately in the lunchboxes. To eat, top half of the toasts with goats' cheese and the rest with beetroot hummus. Serve with the rocket and seeds.

NO-COOK BEETROOT, ORANGE + GINGER SOUP

INGREDIENTS:

10–12 ready-cooked and peeled beetroots
2 oranges (or 250ml orange juice)
about 2 teaspoons honey, to taste
1–2cm piece fresh ginger, to taste

TRY THIS...

· Add a carrot for extra sweetness.

· The soup can be served hot or cold, and it
  works well for breakfast if you want a vegetable
  hit in the morning. To heat, use a microwave
  (about 2 minutes; do not boil).

· If you have a powerful blender you can blitz
  part of the peel and seeds of the orange too.
  The result will be more bitter so you may want
  extra honey.

METHOD:

Put the beetroots in a blender or juicer. Zest and
juice the orange and add along with the honey.
Peel and finely grate half the ginger and add to
the blender.

Blitz for 3–5 minutes until completely smooth.
Top up with water (about 250ml) to reach the
desired consistency. Taste and add more honey
or ginger, if wished.

To pack: Pour into leakproof containers.

AUBERGINE

4 IDEAS FOR BAKED AUBERGINE
WITH CHICKPEAS

1 aubergine
1 x 400g can chickpeas
100g cooked wild rice (optional)
60g baby spinach leaves
coconut/olive oil for drizzling
plus ingredients for one of the flavouring options
  (*see opposite and overleaf*)

Preheat the oven to 200°C and boil a full kettle. Remove the stalk and chop the (unpeeled) aubergine into 2cm cubes. Place in a pan with a pinch of salt, cover with boiled water and cook for 4 minutes until just softening. Drain and place on a baking tray.

Mix with the drained and rinsed chickpeas plus the main ingredients for one of the flavourings. Bake for 20–25 minutes until the chickpeas are slightly crisp and the aubergine is cooked through, stirring every 5 minutes.

Allow to cool before mixing through the rice, if using, plus any extras suggested for the flavouring. Season.

To pack: Spoon into the lunchboxes and pile the spinach on top. Pack the oil separately, to drizzle over before eating.

Tahini, yoghurt and pomegranate

1 garlic clove
1 tablespoon honey
1 tablespoon coconut/olive oil
extra: 1 tablespoon chopped fresh parsley
extra: 1 tablespoon tahini
extra: 1 tablespoon Greek yoghurt
extra: 2 handfuls of pomegranate seeds

Peel and crush the garlic and add to the aubergine with the honey and oil before baking. Stir through the parsley, tahini, yoghurt and pomegranate seeds once the aubergine mix has cooled.

Miso and chilli

juice of 2 limes
1 tablespoon miso paste (mix with a little water so it has a sauce-like consistency)
1 teaspoon dried chilli flakes
2 teaspoons honey
1 tablespoon coconut/olive oil
extra: 1 handful of chopped fresh coriander

Add the lime juice, miso paste, chilli flakes, honey and oil to the aubergine before baking. Stir through the coriander once the aubergine mix has cooled.

Sesame, cranberry and orange

2 oranges
2 tablespoons honey
40g sesame seeds
extra: 40g dried cranberries

Zest and juice the oranges. Add to the aubergine
with the honey and sesame seeds before baking.
Stir through the cranberries once the aubergine
mix has cooled.

Tamarind, almond and ginger

3cm piece fresh ginger
2 tablespoons tamarind paste (or 1 tablespoon
   brown sugar and the juice of 1 lime)
40g flaked almonds
2 teaspoons honey
1 tablespoon coconut/olive oil
extra: 20 fresh mint leaves

Peel and finely grate the ginger, then add
to the aubergine along with the tamarind
paste, almonds, honey and oil before baking.
Stir through the torn mint leaves after the
aubergine mix has cooled.

BABAGANOUSH ON RYE

2 aubergines
coconut/olive oil for drizzling
3 red peppers
4 slices rye bread
1 garlic clove
1 lemon
2 tablespoons tahini
2 tablespoons roughly chopped fresh parsley
60g rocket

Preheat the oven to 220°C and boil a full kettle.

Peel the aubergines. Roughly chop into large chunks. Place in a pan, cover with boiled water and simmer over a medium heat for 3–4 minutes. Drain and place on a baking tray. Toss with a drizzle of oil and sprinkle of salt, then roast for 5–10 minutes until golden.

Meanwhile, prepare the red peppers. Remove the core and seeds, then slice into 2cm-thick wedges. Place on a separate baking tray, drizzle over some oil and season with salt. Roast for 10 minutes.

Toast the rye bread. Very finely chop the garlic; zest and juice the lemon.

Once the aubergine is ready, blitz it in a food processor until just smooth but still with some texture. Stir in the garlic, lemon zest and juice, tahini and parsley. Season.

To pack: Spoon the Babaganoush into a small container. Pack it, the oven-roasted red peppers and rocket separate from the rye bread in the lunchboxes to prevent it from going soggy. To eat, top the rye with the Babaganoush and serve the red pepper and rocket alongside.

RATATOUILLE SALAD

2 aubergines
3 courgettes
olive oil for drizzling
2 handfuls of cherry tomatoes
2 jarred roasted red peppers
1 red onion
4 tablespoons chopped mixed fresh herbs
  (e.g. mint, parsley and chives)
60g mixed crunchy salad leaves
2 tablespoons balsamic vinegar
  (or a home-made glaze, *see below*)

Heat a griddle pan over a very high heat. Meanwhile, slice the aubergines lengthways into thin strips, and cut the courgettes into 1cm-thick rounds. Sear the courgettes and aubergines, in batches, for about a minute until charred on each side. As they are charred, remove them to a bowl. Add a drizzle of olive oil and pinch of salt.

Cut the cherry tomatoes in half. Drain the red peppers and slice into strips. Place these in a separate bowl and season with a pinch of salt.

Peel and finely slice the onion. Add to the tomatoes and red pepper strips along with the chopped herbs.

To pack: Put the charred courgette and aubergine in one third of each lunchbox, the crunchy salad leaves in another third and the cherry tomato mix in the final third. Pack the balsamic vinegar separately, to be poured over the tomatoes, pepper and red onion before eating.

TRY THIS… To make a balsamic glaze, put 4 tablespoons balsamic vinegar in a pan with a little honey and reduce over a low heat until sticky. Wait for the glaze to cool before drizzling over the tomatoes, red pepper and red onion (do this the night before).

AUBERGINE + ALMOND FALAFEL SALAD

INGREDIENTS:

2 aubergines
olive oil for drizzling
about 6 tablespoons ground almonds
1 tablespoon smoked paprika
1 tablespoon plus 1 teaspoon ground cumin
2 x 400g cans chickpeas
200g chopped kale
2 tablespoons pumpkin seeds
1½ tablespoons tahini
4 tablespoons Greek yoghurt
lemon juice

METHOD:

Preheat the oven to 220°C and boil a full kettle.

Prepare, boil and roast the aubergines as for the Babaganoush (*see opposite*). Cool slightly, then tip into a bowl and add the ground almonds, smoked paprika and 1 tablespoon cumin.

Drain and rinse the chickpeas. Put half of them in a food processor and pulse to a chunky consistency. Scrape into the bowl of aubergine. Mix well and season with a pinch of salt. Roll the mix into golfball-sized balls, adding more ground almonds if the mixture is too soft. Place the balls on a parchment-lined baking tray and bake for 10–15 minutes until golden. Once the falafel are in the oven, spread out the remaining chickpeas on another baking tray and toss with a splash of oil, a pinch of salt and the remaining teaspoon of cumin. Roast alongside the falafel for 8–10 minutes. Allow to cool.

Meanwhile, place the kale in a bowl, cover with boiled water and leave for 5 minutes. Drain and rinse under cold water. Set to one side.

Toast the pumpkin seeds in a dry pan for 2 minutes until they start to pop. Make the dressing by mixing together the tahini, yoghurt and lemon juice to taste with a pinch of salt.

To pack: Once all the elements of the salad have cooled, lay the kale along the bottom of the lunchboxes. Top one side with the falafel, and the other side with the roasted chickpeas. Sprinkle the toasted pumpkin seeds over everything. Pack the dressing separately.

TRY THIS…

· Add 2 handfuls of pomegranate seeds (sprinkle on top with the pumpkin seeds) and tuck in a wedge of lime.

· Serve with a chicken breast. Place a skinless, boneless chicken breast on a small baking tray and add a drizzle of oil, some chopped fresh mint and coriander and a pinch of salt. Bake in a preheated 180°C oven for 15–18 minutes. Cool, then slice at an angle before adding to the lunchboxes.

GENERAL CAULIFLOWER NOTES

1. One small to medium cauliflower – roughly
400g once outer leaves and green parts are
removed – creates 2 portions.

2. To make cauli rice, only blitz (on the pulse
setting) a handful at a time for less than 30 seconds.
There will still be a few small chunks. Scoop out the
bits that look like rice and re-blitz what remains
or chop into small pieces.

CAULI-FLOWER

CAULIFLOWER + CHERRY TOMATO SALAD WITH ROMESCO SAUCE

INGREDIENTS:

1 small cauliflower *(see note 1, page 88)*
2 handfuls of cherry tomatoes
2 tablespoons picked fresh parsley leaves

Romesco sauce
2 thick slices day-old bread
80g blanched almonds (flaked work well too)
10 cherry tomatoes
1 teaspoon red wine vinegar
rapeseed oil
2 jarred roasted red peppers

TRY THIS…

· Add 100g cooked Puy lentils or pile a handful of rocket leaves on top.

· Romesco sauce will keep for 3 days in the fridge. Serve as a dip, on toast, over cooked fish or at breakfast with avocado.

· Wrap 2 skinless boneless chicken breasts in Parma ham and roast in a 180°C oven for 15–18 minutes. Serve with a dollop of Romesco and spinach leaves for dinner.

METHOD:

Preheat the oven to 200°C and boil a full kettle. To make the sauce, tear the bread into a few pieces on to a baking tray and add half the nuts and the tomatoes. Mix through the vinegar, a little oil and seasoning. Spread out, then roast for 8–10 minutes until slightly browned all over, stirring every few minutes.

Transfer the roasted ingredients, with any cooking liquid, to a food processor. Add the red peppers, a little more oil and a splash of water. Blitz until combined. Check the seasoning. (You can add extra oil/water and blitz for longer for a smoother texture, if preferred.)

Remove the outer leaves from the cauliflower, then chop (including the base) into small florets and pieces. Put in a pan, cover with boiled water and add a pinch of salt. Cook for 3–5 minutes until al dente. Drain and rinse under cold water.

Mix the cauliflower with the halved cherry tomatoes, parsley and remaining almonds. Add seasoning.

To pack: Divide between the lunchboxes. Pack the sauce separately.

BAKED SALMON, CAULIFLOWER + TOMATO SALAD WITH BASIL DRESSING

INGREDIENTS:

2 salmon fillets, about 150g each
rapeseed oil
40g pine nuts/unsalted cashews
40g mixed seeds
1 small cauliflower *(see note 1, page 88)*
2 handfuls of cherry tomatoes
40g rocket

Basil dressing:
20 fresh basil leaves
juice of 1 lemon
1 tablespoon olive oil

METHOD:

Preheat the oven to 180°C and boil a full kettle. Place the salmon on a baking tray, drizzle over a little oil and season. Sprinkle with the nuts and seeds. Bake for 12 minutes until just cooked. Cool.

While the salmon is in the oven, remove the thick core and outer leaves from the cauliflower. Cut into small florets; cut the stalks into similar-sized chunks. Place in a pan with a pinch of salt and cover with boiled water. Cook for 3–4 minutes until al dente. Drain and rinse under cold water.

Blitz the ingredients for the dressing in a food processor with 1 tablespoon water and season to taste.

Cut the cherry tomatoes in half and mix with the cauliflower. If you like, flake the salmon in large pieces and fold through, or leave the fillets whole.

To pack: Divide the salad between two lunchboxes and top with rocket. Pack the dressing separately.

TRY THIS...

· Swap the salmon for 2 smoked trout or mackerel fillets, flaked (these don't need to be cooked).

· Sprinkle over some crumbled feta.

· Stir 1 tablespoon Green Pesto *(see page 154)* into the dressing.

SPICED CAULIFLOWER WITH PISTACHIOS + MINT

INGREDIENTS:

1 small cauliflower *(see note 1, page 88)*
2 skinless boneless chicken breasts
4cm piece fresh ginger
coconut oil
2 teaspoons ground turmeric/cumin
    (or a mix of the two)
1½ tablespoons honey
50g unsalted pistachios, crushed
fresh mint leaves
lemon juice

METHOD:

Boil a full kettle. Remove the thick core and outer leaves from the cauliflower. Chop the cauliflower into small florets and the stalks into similar-sized chunks. Place in a pan, cover with boiled water and add a pinch of salt. Boil for 3 minutes. Drain well.

Slice the chicken into strips. Peel the ginger and grate into a frying pan. Add a little coconut oil and the turmeric along with the cauliflower and fry over a medium heat for 3–5 minutes until starting to crisp up. Add the chicken and cook, stirring regularly, for a further 5 minutes until cooked through.

Remove from the heat and stir through the honey followed by the pistachios, torn mint leaves and lemon juice to taste. Season.

To pack: Divide between the lunchboxes.

TRY THIS...

· Crumble feta on top.

· Omit the chicken and serve with roast leg of lamb for dinner.

TIP: Gently tear mint or basil leaves instead of chopping as they brown easily when cut.

4 IDEAS FOR CAULI RICE

Green pesto and chicken (facing page, top left)

2 skinless boneless chicken breasts
rapeseed oil
100g frozen peas
1 small cauliflower *(see note 1, page 88)*
2 portions of Green Pesto *(see page 154)*
40g baby spinach leaves
lemon juice/olive oil
freshly grated Parmesan (optional)

Chop the chicken into thin strips and place in a large frying pan with a little oil and seasoning. Fry over a medium heat for 5 minutes, stirring frequently, until cooked through and slightly browned. Remove from the pan.

While the chicken is cooking, thaw the peas in a bowl of cold water for 1–2 minutes; drain.

Remove the thick core and outer leaves from the cauliflower. Chop the cauliflower into 2cm chunks, then blitz in small batches until it resembles rice *(see note 2, page 88)*.

Place the cauli rice in the frying pan with a little more oil and cook over a medium-high heat for 3 minutes, stirring regularly. The cauli rice should be just cooked but still crunchy and slightly crisp in parts. Cool.

Stir the pesto, peas, spinach and chicken through the cauli rice. Season and add a little lemon juice or a drizzle of olive oil to taste.

To pack: Divide between the lunchboxes and garnish with a sprinkle of Parmesan, if you like.

Red pepper pesto (facing page, top right)

1 small cauliflower *(see note 1, page 92)*
rapeseed oil
4 sun-dried tomatoes
2 jarred roasted red peppers
2 portions of Red Pepper Pesto *(see page 155)*
lemon juice
40g rocket

Remove the thick core and outer leaves from the cauliflower. Chop the cauliflower into 2cm chunks, then blitz in small batches until it resembles rice *(see note 2, page 92)*.

Place in a frying pan with a little oil and cook over a medium-high heat for 3 minutes, stirring regularly, until the cauli rice is just cooked through but still crunchy and slightly crisp. Cool.

Finely slice the sun-dried tomatoes and red peppers. Mix with the cauli rice and pesto. Season and add a little olive oil and lemon juice to taste.

To pack: Divide between the lunchboxes and top with the rocket.

Nutty Mushroom

1 small cauliflower *(see note 1, page 88)*
rapeseed oil
1 teaspoon ground coriander
40g hazelnuts
2 garlic cloves
250g chestnut mushrooms
1 tablespoon finely chopped fresh thyme
50g Parmesan
40g rocket
4 fresh figs (dried figs work well too)

Remove the thick core and outer leaves from the cauliflower. Chop the cauliflower into 2cm chunks, then blitz in small batches until it resembles rice *(see note 2, page 88)*. Place the cauli rice in a frying pan with a little rapeseed oil and cook over a medium-high heat for 3 minutes, stirring regularly. The cauli rice should be just cooked but still crunchy and slightly crisp in parts. Tip into a bowl and set aside.

Wipe the pan dry, then lightly toast the coriander and hazelnuts in the pan over a medium heat for 2 minutes, stirring constantly. Tip into a small bowl and set aside.

Peel and finely chop the garlic. Place in the frying pan with a splash more oil and cook over a medium heat for 1 minute. Finely dice three-quarters of the mushrooms and cut the remaining mushrooms in half. Add them all to the pan along with the coriander and hazelnuts and the thyme. Cook over a medium-high heat for 2 minutes, stirring regularly.

Add the cauli rice to the pan and mix through. Grate over the Parmesan. Cook everything together for a final 2–4 minutes, stirring. Season.

To pack: Divide between the lunchboxes. Pile the rocket on top along with the quartered figs.

TRY THIS...

Oven-roast the quartered figs with a drizzle of honey.

Kale and walnut pesto with salmon

150g chopped kale
1 small cauliflower *(see note 1, page 88)*
rapeseed oil
2 portions of Kale and Walnut Pesto
   (see page 155)
lemon juice
2 salmon fillets, about 150g each
50g walnut halves

Boil a full kettle. Place the kale in a bowl and cover with boiled water. Leave for 5 minutes, then drain and rinse under cold water. Set aside.

Remove the thick core and outer leaves from the cauliflower. Chop the cauliflower into 2cm chunks, then blitz in small batches until it resembles rice *(see note 2, page 88)*.

Place in a frying pan with a little oil and cook over a medium-high heat for 3 minutes, stirring regularly, until the cauli rice is just cooked through but still crunchy and slightly crisp in parts. Tip into a bowl.

Stir the pesto and kale through the cauli rice. Season and add oil and lemon juice to taste.

Wipe the pan clean and heat a little more oil. Remove the skin from the salmon and cut into roughly 2cm chunks. Fry over a medium heat for 2 minutes until just cooked. Add to the cauli rice.

Crush the walnuts (or leave them whole) and toast in the frying pan for 2 minutes until lightly golden. Mix into the salad.

To pack: Divide between the lunchboxes.

TRY THIS…

Swap the cauli rice for 140g cooked quinoa, pasta or brown rice.

CAULIFLOWER, HARISSA + ALMOND SOUP

INGREDIENTS:

1 red onion

rapeseed oil

¼ teaspoon ground cinnamon

½ teaspoon ground cumin

1 small cauliflower *(see note 1, page 88)*

1 garlic clove

100g toasted flaked almonds, plus optional extra
  to garnish

500ml vegetable, beef or chicken stock

4–6 teaspoons harissa paste

TRY THIS...

· Add drained canned butter beans/cooked diced
  chicken after blitzing, and finish with crumbled
  feta and chopped parsley.

· Top with a dollop of Greek yoghurt or soured
  cream.

METHOD:

Peel and finely slice the onion. Fry with a little
oil in a medium-sized pan over a low heat for
10 minutes until completely soft. Turn up the
heat, add the spices and fry for a further
2 minutes until very fragrant.

While the onion is softening, remove the outer
leaves from the cauliflower and roughly chop
(including the base) into small pieces. Add to the
pan and cook, stirring regularly, for 5 minutes until
browned. You may need to add a little more oil.

Peel and crush the garlic, then add to the pan
along with the almonds. Fry for 2 more minutes.
Pour in the stock – if it doesn't cover the
vegetables completely, top up with boiling water.
Bring to the boil, then simmer for 10 minutes
until the cauliflower is very tender. Stir through
the harissa (to taste) and cool.

Blitz in a food processor until smooth, diluting
with extra water, if needed, to reach a soup
consistency. Season to taste. You may want to
add a little more harissa or a squeeze of lemon
juice at the end.

To pack: Split the soup between two leakproof
containers. Pack extra flaked almonds separately
if you want to garnish the soup. Serve warm.

TIP: Make a double batch and freeze half in individual portions.

CABBAGE

RED CABBAGE, APPLE + TAHINI SLAW WITH SALMON + BEETROOT

INGREDIENTS:

2 salmon fillets, about 150g each
rapeseed oil
40g sesame seeds
2 apples
1 lemon
½ red cabbage
1 tablespoon chopped fresh coriander
1½ tablespoons tahini
4 ready-cooked and peeled beetroots

METHOD:

Preheat the oven to 180°C. Place the salmon on a baking tray. Drizzle over a little oil and season with salt and pepper. Bake for 12 minutes until cooked through. After 5 minutes, sprinkle the sesame seeds on to the baking tray alongside the salmon so they can lightly toast. Allow to cool.

While the salmon is baking, quarter the apples and remove the cores, then grate into a sieve. Press out any excess liquid. Tip the apple into a medium-sized bowl. Zest the lemon on to the apple and squeeze in the juice. Toss well.

Remove the hard outer leaves and core from the cabbage. Grate or finely slice the cabbage. Add to the apple along with the coriander, tahini and a drizzle of oil. Mix well and season.

Slice the beetroots into quarters.

To pack: Spread the slaw in the lunchboxes. Place the salmon on top to one side and sprinkle with the toasted sesame seeds. Place the beetroot on the other side.

TRY THIS...

· Add a dollop of Greek yoghurt for a creamier slaw.

· Swap the apples for carrots.

FENNEL, ORANGE, CHICKEN + HAZELNUT CABBAGE SLAW

INGREDIENTS:

2 skinless boneless chicken breasts
rapeseed oil
1 fennel bulb
½ red cabbage
2 oranges
1 tablespoon honey
1 tablespoon finely chopped fresh parsley/chives
60g hazelnuts

TRY THIS…

· Add a 400g can of chickpeas, drained and rinsed, for extra protein, or instead of the chicken.

· Swap the orange for grapefruit, or peach pieces with added lemon juice.

· Sprinkle with crumbled feta.

METHOD:

Preheat the oven to 180°C. Place the chicken on a baking tray and drizzle over a little oil. Season. Bake for 15–18 minutes until cooked through. Cool, then thinly slice (or leave whole).

While the chicken is cooking, remove the hard outer pieces/leaves from the fennel and cabbage. Cut out the cabbage core. Finely shred the fennel and cabbage with a knife and place in a bowl.

Cut one orange in half and squeeze the juice over the fennel and cabbage. Peel the other orange and separate into segments. Add to the bowl along with the chicken, honey, herbs and a drizzle of oil. Mix well and season to taste.

To pack: Spoon into the lunchboxes. Coarsely crush the nuts and sprinkle on top.

TOFU PAD THAI

INGREDIENTS:

100g tofu
120ml soy sauce
½ red cabbage
lemon juice
4 carrots
160g sugarsnap peas
140g glass noodles
2 tablespoons honey (optional)
2 tablespoons chopped fresh coriander
40g toasted sesame seeds/unsalted peanuts

TRY THIS…

· Pickle the red cabbage – half an hour ahead,
  marinate it in 4 tablespoons each white wine
  vinegar, vegetable oil and honey, then drain.

· Sprinkle over some cooked prawns at the end.

· Instead of dressing the noodles with the
  reduced soy sauce, use our Peanut Teriyaki
  Sauce (*see page 156*).

METHOD:

Preheat the oven to 180°C and boil a full kettle.

Cut the tofu into 3cm cubes. Place in a bowl with
the soy sauce – the tofu cubes should be covered.
Leave to marinate for 10 minutes.

Meanwhile, remove the coarse outer leaves and
core from the red cabbage. Grate and place in a
bowl. Toss with a squeeze of lemon juice to keep
fresh. Peel and spiralise the carrots.

Slice the sugarsnap peas in half lengthways, on
the diagonal. Cover with boiled water and leave
for 2 minutes. Drain and immediately tip into a
bowl of cold water, then drain again. Set aside.

Put the glass noodles in a pan, cover with boiled
water and simmer for 3–5 minutes until just
cooked. Drain and rinse under cold water.
Place in a bowl and snip up roughly with scissors
(smaller pieces will be easier to eat at your desk).

While the noodles are cooking, drain the soy
sauce from the tofu into a pan and reduce over
a low heat until sticky. Cool, then toss into the
noodles. Sweeten with honey, if you like.

Line a baking tray with baking parchment
and lay out the marinated tofu cubes. Bake for
10 minutes until golden, turning the tofu halfway
through. Cool.

Mix the coriander through the noodles, along
with the sesame seeds or peanuts.

To pack: Place the noodles, carrots, cabbage and
sugarsnaps in separate sections in the lunchboxes
and dot the tofu on top.

CABBAGE CARAWAY CHICKEN SALAD

INGREDIENTS:

2 skinless boneless chicken breasts
4 tablespoons finely chopped fresh parsley
2 tablespoons rapeseed oil
$\frac{1}{2}$ red cabbage
$\frac{1}{4}$ white cabbage
2 teaspoons caraway seeds
1 lemon
2 tablespoons Dijon mustard
1 tablespoon cider vinegar
60g rocket

TRY THIS...

Add some cucumber moons for extra crunch –
cut cucumber in half lengthways and scoop out
the seeds with a spoon, then slice across to create
1cm-thick moons.

METHOD:

Preheat the oven to 180°C. Place the chicken
on a baking tray. Mix the parsley with the oil to
form a green paste. Spread over the chicken and
season. Bake for 15–18 minutes until just cooked.
Allow to cool, then slice at an angle.

While the chicken is in the oven, remove the
tough outer leaves and core from the cabbages.
Grate and place in a bowl.

Lightly toast the caraway seeds in a small
dry pan over a medium heat for 3 minutes.
Zest the lemon. Add to the cabbage along with
the caraway seeds, mustard, vinegar and some
lemon juice, if you like. Toss together well.

To pack: Spoon the cabbage into the lunchboxes
and add the chicken. Pile the rocket on top.

CHICKEN AIOLI SALAD

INGREDIENTS:

2 skinless boneless chicken breasts
2 lemons
4 tablespoons mixed seeds
rapeseed oil
150g mixed wild and long-grain rice
100g frozen peas
½ red or white cabbage (or mix of ¼ red
and ¼ white, which is prettier)
1 garlic clove
4 tablespoons Greek yoghurt

METHOD:

Preheat the oven to 180°C and boil a full kettle. Place the chicken on a baking tray. Zest the lemons and sprinkle over the chicken along with the mixed seeds, a drizzle of oil and a pinch of salt. Bake for 15–18 minutes. Allow to cool, then slice at an angle.

While the chicken is in the oven, put the rice in a pan, cover with boiled water and add a pinch of salt. Simmer over a medium heat for 12–14 minutes until al dente. Drain. Place in a bowl, season and stir through the peas.

Remove the tough outer leaves and core from the cabbage, then finely slice.

To make the dressing, peel and finely chop the garlic, then mix with the yoghurt, the juice from one lemon and a pinch of salt.

To pack: Spoon the rice into one half of each lunchbox and the cabbage in the other. Fan the sliced chicken across the rice. Tuck in a wedge of lemon. Pack the dressing separately.

PEAR, BACON, CABBAGE + ROCKET SALAD

INGREDIENTS:	METHOD:

INGREDIENTS:

2 pears
4 streaky bacon rashers
60g walnuts/pecans (flaked almonds also
    work well)
2 tablespoons honey
½ white cabbage
2 teaspoons Dijon or wholegrain mustard
    (or lemon juice to taste)
2 tablespoons cider vinegar
2 tablespoons rapeseed oil
30g rocket

METHOD:

Preheat the oven to 200°C. Peel the pears and
slice into quarters lengthways. Remove the core,
then slice each quarter in half lengthways so
you have 16 pieces in all. Place on a baking tray.

Cut the bacon rashers across into strips and
pile on the tray. Crush the nuts and mix with
the bacon along with the honey. Spread out
the bacon in a single layer. Bake both trays
for 10–12 minutes, stirring every few minutes,
until the bacon is cooked. The pear should
still be quite firm. Allow to cool.

Meanwhile, remove the tough outer cabbage
leaves and the core, then grate the cabbage.
Whisk the mustard with the vinegar and oil,
then thoroughly mix through the cabbage.

Add the pears and bacon and season.

To pack: Spoon the salad into the lunchboxes
and top with the rocket.

TRY THIS...

· Scatter crumbled blue or goats' cheese on
  top before the rocket, or add a dollop of
  crème fraîche.

· Serve the baked pears and bacon on sourdough
  toast with Greek yoghurt for brunch.

3 IDEAS FOR COURGETTI
POT NOODLES

Thai green pot

100g frozen shelled edamame beans
3 courgettes
100g green beans
100g chopped kale
100g sugarsnap peas
1–4 teaspoons Thai green curry paste (add more
    or less depending on how spicy you want it)

Thaw the edamame in a bowl of cold water
for 1–2 minutes, then drain. Meanwhile, trim
the courgettes, then spiralise into courgetti
(alternatively, shave into ribbons with a peeler,
discarding the watery centre). Trim the green
beans and slice into 1cm rounds.

To pack: Split all the ingredients between the
lunchboxes (or heatproof jars). Before eating,
boil a kettle, then add 250ml boiled water to
the ingredients. Stir and leave for 2–3 minutes
before eating.

TRY THIS…

Garnish with a handful of toasted flaked
almonds, packed separately.

Tofu pho

4 courgettes
100g tofu
2cm piece fresh ginger
2 spring onions (white bulbs and most
    of the green)
100g beansprouts
15 fresh mint leaves
2 vegetable stock cubes
soy sauce/sweet chilli sauce (optional)
lime wedges

Trim the courgettes, then spiralise into courgetti
(alternatively, shave into ribbons with a peeler,
discarding the watery centre). Cut the tofu into
cubes. Peel and finely dice the ginger. Slice the
spring onions.

To pack: Split all the prepared ingredients
between the lunchboxes (or heatproof jars).
Add the beansprouts, mint and crumbled stock
cube. Before serving, boil a kettle, then add
250ml boiled water to the ingredients. Stir and
leave for 2–3 minutes. Season with a little soy
sauce or sweet chilli sauce, if you like, and lime
juice to taste (pack the wedges separately).

Rainbow pot

100g frozen shelled edamame beans
3 courgettes
2 carrots
3cm piece fresh ginger
2 spring onions (white bulbs only)
2 vegetable stock cubes
150g chopped kale
2 handfuls of beansprouts
1 tablespoon chopped fresh coriander
soy sauce or sweet chilli sauce (optional)

Thaw the edamame in a bowl of cold water for 1–2 minutes; drain. Meanwhile, trim the courgettes, then spiralise into courgetti (alternatively, shave into ribbons with a peeler, discarding the watery centre). Peel and spiralise the carrots. Peel and grate the ginger. Finely slice the spring onion bulbs.

To pack: Crumble a stock cube into each lunchbox (or heatproof jar). Add the prepared ingredients along with the kale, beansprouts, coriander and edamame beans. Before eating, boil a kettle, then add 250ml boiled water to the ingredients. Stir and leave for 2–3 minutes. Season with a little soy sauce or sweet chilli sauce, if you like.

TRY THIS…

· Add leftover roast chicken, cut into small pieces, or a few squares of tofu.

· Spice up the pot noodle by adding a teaspoon of curry paste (tikka, green or red all work well).

COURGETTI + RED PEPPER PESTO

INGREDIENTS:

3 courgettes
1 fresh red chilli
1 red pepper
1 x 400g can butter beans
40g unsalted cashews
1 mozzarella ball (or a handful of mini ones)
light olive oil
2 portions of Red Pepper Pesto *(see page 155)*
40g rocket

TRY THIS…

Add mini turkey meatballs – mix together
200g turkey mince, 2 teaspoons garlic granules,
1 tablespoon finely chopped fresh parsley and
the zest of ½ lemon. Season. Roll into small
golf balls. Place on a baking tray and bake in
a preheated 180°C oven for 10–12 minutes.

METHOD:

Trim the courgettes, then spiralise into courgetti
(alternatively, shave into ribbons with a peeler,
discarding the watery centre.)

Cut the chilli in half lengthways and remove the
seeds using a teaspoon, then finely dice. Remove
the core and seeds from the red pepper, then slice
into thin strips.

Drain and rinse the butter beans. Place in a bowl
and mix through the chilli (to taste), red pepper,
cashews, torn mozzarella and a splash of oil.
Season.

To pack: Pile the courgetti in one side of the
lunchboxes and top with a dollop of pesto.
Spoon the bean salad on the other side of
the lunchboxes and top with rocket.

COURGETTI WITH KALE + WALNUT PESTO-BAKED SALMON

INGREDIENTS:

2 salmon fillets, about 150g each
2 portions of Kale and Walnut Pesto
  (see page 155)
2 handfuls of cherry tomatoes
rapeseed oil
3 courgettes
80g watercress

TRY THIS...

Spiralise beetroot or butternut squash instead
of courgettes, toss with a little oil and bake in
a 180°C oven for 10 minutes.

METHOD:

Preheat the oven to 180°C and boil a full kettle.
Line a baking tray with baking parchment. Place
the salmon on one side of the tray. Spread the pesto
across the top of the salmon, ensuring the fillets
are completely covered. Bake for 12 minutes until
cooked through. Halfway through cooking, scatter
the cherry tomatoes on the other side of the tray,
drizzle them with a little oil and sprinkle with salt.

Meanwhile, trim the courgettes, then spiralise
into courgetti (alternatively, shave into ribbons
with a peeler, discarding the watery centre).

To pack: Spread the courgetti in the lunchboxes.
Once the salmon and tomatoes have cooled,
flake the salmon and scatter over the top with
the tomatoes and watercress.

RIBBONED COURGETTE SALAD WITH THAI FISHCAKES

INGREDIENTS:

Fishcakes
100g peeled sweet potato
50g green beans
2 skinless salmon fillets, about 150g each
2 tablespoons Thai green curry paste
30g desiccated coconut

Salad
12 asparagus spears
3 courgettes
juice of 1 lemon

TRY THIS...

· Serve with sweet chilli sauce or crème fraîche.

· Swap the salmon for mackerel or cod fillet.

METHOD:

Preheat the oven to 180°C and boil a full kettle.

Make the fishcakes first. Cut the sweet potato into 2cm chunks. Place in a pan with a pinch of salt, cover with boiled water and cook for 6–8 minutes until just soft. Drain. Mash until smooth with a potato masher or fork.

While the sweet potato is cooking, trim the green beans and cut into 1cm pieces. Place in a bowl, cover with boiled water and leave for 4 minutes, then drain. Slice the asparagus spears for the salad in half lengthways and place in another bowl. Cover with boiled water and leave for 3 minutes, then drain.

Dice the salmon and place in a blender with the curry paste. Blitz until smooth. Mix through the mashed sweet potato and season. Add the green beans. Shape the mix into 4–6 balls and press each down to form an oval cake. Dip both sides in desiccated coconut to coat. Place the coated fishcakes on a baking tray lined with greaseproof paper and bake for 12–15 minutes, turning over halfway through, until golden brown.

Meanwhile, make the salad. Trim the courgettes, then shave into ribbons using a vegetable peeler. Toss with the asparagus, lemon juice and a little salt.

To pack: Split the salad between the lunchboxes. Once the fishcakes are cool, lay them on top of the salad.

COURGETTI + SWEET POTATO SALAD WITH AVOCADO DRESSING

INGREDIENTS:

2 sweet potatoes
3 courgettes
60g unsalted cashews
2 handfuls of pomegranate seeds
10 fresh basil leaves

Dressing
¼ avocado
20g unsalted cashews
2 teaspoons cider vinegar
1 tablespoon light olive oil

METHOD:

Boil a full kettle. Peel the sweet potatoes and cut into 2cm cubes. Place in a pan, cover with boiled water and add a pinch of salt. Simmer for 6–8 minutes until cooked through. Drain and rinse in cold water to cool quickly.

While the sweet potatoes are cooking, trim the courgettes, then spiralise into courgetti (alternatively, shave into ribbons with a peeler, discarding the watery centre). Toast the cashews for the salad in a dry pan until lightly golden.

Blitz all the ingredients for the dressing together in a food processor or blender. Season to taste and loosen with a little water, if necessary.

To pack: Divide the courgetti and sweet potato between the lunchboxes and sprinkle with the pomegranate seeds, torn basil and toasted cashews. Pack the dressing separately.

TRY THIS…

· Add 1 teaspoon harissa paste or tahini to the dressing, or a handful of chopped fresh herbs (basil/parsley/coriander).

· Make the dressing a dip by adding a dollop of natural yoghurt, extra cashews and avocado.

GREEN PESTO-BAKED SALMON WITH CUCUMBER + COURGETTE RIBBONS

INGREDIENTS:

2 salmon fillets, about 150g each
2 portions of Green Pesto *(see page 154)*
2 courgettes
1 cucumber
light olive oil
2 teaspoons snipped fresh dill (or chives)
60g rocket (or mixed leaves)
2 tablespoons mixed seeds (optional)

METHOD:

Preheat the oven to 180°C. Place the salmon on a baking tray. Spread the pesto across the top of each fillet, then bake for 12 minutes. Remove and cool.

Meanwhile, trim the courgettes and cucumber. Use a peeler to shave them both into ribbons, discarding the inner watery part. Place the ribbons in a bowl. Add a light splash of oil, the chopped dill and some salt and toss together.

To pack: Pile the courgette and cucumber ribbons in one half of the lunchboxes and the rocket in the other half. Lay the salmon diagonally across the rocket and ribbons. Sprinkle over the mixed seeds.

TRY THIS…

Swap the salmon for tofu and Tenderstem broccoli. Cut 200g tofu into cubes and 6 stems of broccoli into similar-sized chunks. Mix with the pesto and bake in a 180°C oven for 15–18 minutes until the broccoli is al dente.

GREEN
BEANS

CRUNCHY OAT-SESAME CHICKEN + GREEN BEAN SALAD

INGREDIENTS:

200g green beans
2 skinless boneless chicken breasts
rapeseed oil
25g porridge oats
25g sesame seeds
2 teaspoons dried Italian herbs
1 tablespoon honey
2 teaspoons toasted sesame oil
40g rocket

METHOD:

Boil a full kettle. Trim the green beans, then place in a pan, cover with boiled water and add a pinch of salt. Cook for 3–4 minutes until al dente. Drain and rinse under cold water.

Cut the chicken into small strips. Place in a pan with a splash of oil. Cook, stirring regularly, for 5 minutes until golden and cooked through. Remove from the pan.

Add a little more oil to the pan along with the oats, sesame seeds and Italian herbs. Fry over a medium heat, stirring, for 3–5 minutes until golden brown. Remove from the heat and stir through the honey, sesame oil, green beans and chicken.

To pack: Cool, then spoon the salad into the lunchboxes and top with the rocket.

TRY THIS...

· Add a handful of sweet potato wedges roasted with a little oil in a 200°C oven for 30 minutes, tossed every 10 minutes.

· Swap the sesame seeds or oats for desiccated coconut.

GOATS' CHEESE-STUFFED FIGS

INGREDIENTS:

4 fresh figs
60g goats' cheese
4 slices Parma ham
2 tablespoons olive oil, plus extra for drizzling
60g walnuts
1 tablespoon honey, plus extra for drizzling
200g green beans
40g mixed salad leaves
1 tablespoon balsamic vinegar (or 2 teaspoons
   wholegrain/Dijon mustard)

TRY THIS…

· Swap the goats' cheese for mascarpone/cream
  cheese/feta.

· If figs aren't in season, you can use pears.
  Or simply sprinkle crumbled goats' cheese
  and strips of Parma ham over the beans and
  leaves and add 4 sliced dried figs or apricots.

· Switch to a quick blue cheese dressing. Gently
  melt 40g blue cheese in a pan with a splash
  of milk/cream and olive oil. Season and add
  lemon juice to taste. Cool before packing.

METHOD:

Preheat the oven to 180°C and boil a full kettle.

Place the figs on a baking tray and cut a cross
on the top of each to open it up slightly. Split
the goats' cheese among the figs, squashing it
into the centre. Wrap each fig with a slice of
Parma ham. Drizzle with oil and season.

Bake for 12–15 minutes until the figs are slightly
oozing and the ham is crisp. About 3 minutes
before the figs have finished cooking, add the
nuts to the tray and drizzle with a little honey.

While the figs are in the oven, trim the green
beans and cut in half. Place in a pan, cover with
boiled water and add a pinch of salt. Boil for
4 minutes until al dente. Drain and rinse under
cold water (this will keep them green and prevent
further cooking). Mix with the salad leaves.

Whisk together the 2 tablespoons olive oil,
1 tablespoon honey and vinegar to make a
dressing. Season.

To pack: Spread the salad leaves and green
beans on the bottom of the lunchboxes and
set the cooled figs and honeyed walnuts on top.
Pack the dressing separately.

COCONUT CHICKEN + TAMARIND SALAD

INGREDIENTS:

2 skinless boneless chicken breasts
200g green beans
100g sugarsnap peas (or frozen shelled
    edamame beans)
100g frozen peas
20 fresh basil leaves
30g desiccated coconut

Tamarind dressing
1 tablespoon rapeseed oil,
    plus extra for drizzling
2 tablespoons tamarind paste
juice of 1 lime

METHOD:

Preheat the oven to 180°C and boil a full kettle.
Place the chicken on a baking tray, drizzle
with a little rapeseed oil and season. Bake for
15–18 minutes until cooked through. Allow to
cool, then slice into strips.

While the chicken is in the oven, trim the green
beans, place in a pan and cover with boiled
water. Add a pinch of salt. Cook for 5 minutes
until al dente. Drain and rinse under cold water.

Put the sugarsnap peas in a bowl and cover with
boiled water. Leave for 2 minutes, then drain and
rinse under cold water. Thaw the frozen peas
(and edamame, if using, in a bowl of cold water
for 1–2 minutes; drain. Mix the sugarsnaps and
peas with the green beans and torn basil.

Toast the coconut in a dry pan over a medium
heat until golden brown.

Whisk the dressing ingredients together with
1 tablespoon water and seasoning to taste.

To pack: Spoon the salad into the lunchboxes,
top with the chicken slices and sprinkle the toasted
coconut on top. Pack the dressing separately.

TRY THIS…

· Add a sliced fresh red chilli for some heat.

· Buy unsweetened desiccated coconut if you can
  as it has a natural unsweetened flavour.

· Toast a bigger batch of coconut and use the
  rest as a breakfast topper stirred through Greek
  yoghurt or mixed through muesli.

PEANUT TERIYAKI GREEN BEANS + TOFU

INGREDIENTS:

100g mixed wild and long-grain rice
200g tofu
2 teaspoons cornflour
3 tablespoons toasted sesame oil (or rapeseed oil)
200g green beans
120g frozen shelled edamame beans
2 portions of Peanut Teriyaki Sauce *(see page 156)*

TRY THIS...

Swap the tofu for salmon. Double the teriyaki sauce and spoon half over 2 salmon fillets, then bake in a 180°C oven for 12 minutes until just cooked through. Flake through the salad.

METHOD:

Preheat the oven to 180°C and boil a full kettle. Put the rice in a pan with a pinch of salt and cover with boiled water. Boil for 15–18 minutes until al dente. Drain.

While the rice is cooking, briefly drain the tofu on kitchen paper, then cut into 3cm cubes. Put the tofu in a bowl with the cornflour and sesame oil. Gently toss together, ensuring the tofu cubes are completely covered by the cornflour. Spread out on a baking tray lined with a sheet of baking parchment and bake for 15 minutes until golden brown. Flip the tofu cubes over halfway through cooking.

Boil another kettle. Trim the green beans, then place in a pan, cover with boiled water and add a pinch of salt. Cook for 5 minutes, then drain and rinse under cold water.

Thaw the edamame beans in a bowl of cold water for 1–2 minutes; drain.

To pack: Spoon the vegetables and rice into the lunchboxes and sprinkle the tofu on top. Pack the sauce separately. To eat, mix the sauce through the tofu: the cornflour will absorb the flavours.

THAI BAKED HALLOUMI SALAD

INGREDIENTS:

120g halloumi cheese (or tofu/feta)
2 teaspoons Thai green curry paste
juice of ½ lemon
80g unsalted cashews
150g green beans
4 spring onions (white bulbs and most
    of the green)
50g baby spinach leaves

Dressing
1–2 teaspoons Thai green curry paste
juice of ½ lemon
2 teaspoons honey
2 tablespoons olive oil

TRY THIS…

· Fry 2 handfuls of raw peeled prawns in a
  teaspoon of Thai green curry paste until pink.
  Cool, then add to the bean salad.

· Add 2 handfuls of pomegranate seeds/dried
  cranberries and a chopped avocado dressed
  with lime juice.

METHOD:

Preheat the oven to 200°C and boil a full kettle.
Slice the halloumi into 1cm strips and place on
a sheet of foil on a baking tray. Spread with the
curry paste and lemon juice, then wrap into a
parcel. Cook in the oven for 5 minutes.

Add the cashews to the baking tray alongside the
foil parcel and cook for another 5 minutes until
golden brown. Cool.

While the cheese is in the oven, trim the green
beans, then place in a pan with a pinch of salt
and cover with boiled water. Cook for 4 minutes
until al dente. Drain and rinse under cold water.
Finely slice the spring onions.

Whisk the ingredients for the dressing together,
adding curry paste to taste (depending on how
spicy you like it).

To pack: Spread the green beans in the
lunchboxes and lay the halloumi on top followed
by the spring onions, spinach and nuts. Pack the
dressing separately.

MEXICAN GREEN BEANS

INGREDIENTS:

200g green beans
100g frozen shelled edamame beans
1 x 400g can kidney beans
1 tablespoon cumin seeds
1 x 340g can sweetcorn
rapeseed oil
2 red peppers
4 spring onions (white bulbs and most of the green)
1 tablespoon chopped fresh coriander (optional)

TRY THIS…

· Add some leftover cooked chicken – shred with
  two forks, then toss with a little olive oil, salt
  and chopped fresh coriander. Toast 2 teaspoons
  smoked paprika or ground cumin in a dry pan
  for 3 minutes, then stir through.

· Mix in 80g cooked quinoa or bulghur wheat.

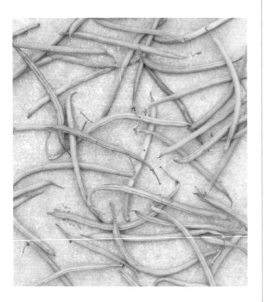

METHOD:

Boil a full kettle. Trim the green beans and
cut into quarters. Place in a pan, cover with
boiled water and add a pinch of salt. Cook for
5 minutes, then drain and rinse under cold water.
Tip into a bowl.

Thaw the edamame beans in a bowl of cold
water for 1–2 minutes; drain. Drain and rinse the
kidney beans. Add both beans to the green beans
in the bowl.

Grind the cumin seeds to a powder in a pestle
and mortar (or use ready-ground cumin). Drain
and rinse the sweetcorn. Place in a pan with a
splash of oil, the cumin and a pinch of salt. Cook
over a medium-high heat, stirring, for 2–3 minutes
until the sweetcorn begins to colour and the
cumin is very fragrant. Cool.

Remove the core and seeds from the red peppers,
then slice into 2cm-thick strips. Finely slice the
spring onions. Add the peppers, sweetcorn and
spring onions to the bowl of beans and toss well
to mix. Add a little oil and seasoning.

To pack: Spoon the salad into the lunchboxes and
sprinkle the coriander on top.

GREEN BEAN MINESTRONE

INGREDIENTS:

1 leek
1 garlic clove (optional)
rapeseed oil
2 carrots
120g chopped kale
2 teaspoons smoked paprika
1 vegetable stock cube
100g orzo pasta
2 tablespoons fresh basil, torn
200g green beans

TRY THIS...

· Add a handful of grated Parmesan before
  packing the soup.

· Swap the pasta for rice.

METHOD:

Finely slice the leek. Peel and finely chop the
garlic (if using). Place both in a pan with a little
oil and a pinch of salt. Cook over a medium heat
for 3 minutes until soft, stirring regularly.

Meanwhile, peel the carrots and dice into 5mm
pieces. Add to the pan and cook for a further
3 minutes.

Add the kale along with the smoked paprika,
crumbled stock cube, pasta and basil. Pour in
900ml water. Trim the green beans and cut in
half, then add to the pan. Bring to the boil and
simmer for about 8 minutes until the pasta is al
dente. Season.

To pack: Allow the minestrone to cool before
packing in leakproof containers. Reheat to serve.

BROCCOLI

BROCCOLI + RED PESTO LENTILS

INGREDIENTS:

150g Puy lentils
200g Tenderstem broccoli
10 cherry tomatoes
2 jarred roasted red peppers
olive oil
lemon (optional)
10 fresh basil leaves
50g goats' cheese/toasted pine nuts (optional)
2 portions of Red Pepper Pesto *(see page 155)*

METHOD:

Boil a full kettle. Put the lentils in a pan with a pinch of salt and cover with boiled water. Cook for 12–15 minutes until al dente. Drain.

While the lentils are cooking, trim the ends from the broccoli and slice the stems in half on an angle, then put into another pan. Add a pinch of salt and cover with boiled water, then cook for 4–5 minutes until al dente. Drain and rinse under cold water.

Cut the cherry tomatoes in half. Cut the red peppers into thin strips.

Put the lentils in a bowl and dress with a little olive oil and seasoning plus lemon zest/juice if you like.

To pack: When the lentils and broccoli are cool, spread the lentils in the lunchboxes. Arrange everything else on top in sections, then sprinkle with torn basil and goats' cheese/pine nuts, if using. Pack the pesto separately. Alternatively, mix everything together before packing.

TRY THIS…

Double the pesto and mix half of it through 2 chopped skinless boneless chicken breasts, then bake these in a 180°C oven for 13–15 minutes until cooked through. Sprinkle the chicken over the lentils and vegetables.

MUSHROOM + PEA PASTA
WITH BROCCOLI SAUCE

INGREDIENTS:

200g shell pasta (conchiglie)
1 medium head of broccoli
2 garlic cloves
150g chestnut mushrooms
rapeseed oil
80g frozen peas
100g crème fraîche
1 tablespoon finely chopped fresh parsley
1 lemon

METHOD:

Boil a full kettle. Put the pasta in a pan with a pinch of salt and cover with boiled water. Cook for 12–14 minutes until al dente. Drain, reserving 100ml of the pasta water.

While the pasta is cooking, cut off the broccoli florets and cut the stalk into similar-sized pieces. Put the stalk pieces in a pan with a pinch of salt and cover with boiled water. Cook for 1 minute, then add the florets and cook for a further 2–3 minutes until al dente. Drain and rinse under cold water.

Peel and finely chop the garlic. Quarter the mushrooms. Put the garlic in a pan with a splash of oil and fry over a low heat for 2 minutes. Add half the broccoli, the mushrooms and peas. Cook over a high heat for 5 minutes, stirring frequently. Remove from the heat.

Combine the crème fraîche, reserved pasta water, parsley and remaining broccoli in a food processor. Blitz until smooth to make a thick sauce. Stir the sauce into the pasta along with the peas and mushrooms. Zest the lemon into the pasta and season to taste with the juice, salt and pepper.

To pack: Spoon into your lunchboxes.

TRY THIS… Add a cooked and flaked fillet of salmon.

SMOKY BROCCOLI + BACON SALAD

INGREDIENTS:

4 smoked streaky bacon rashers
60g flaked almonds
1 medium head of broccoli
rapeseed oil
2 teaspoons smoked paprika
2 teaspoons honey (optional)
2 red peppers
50g rocket
lemon wedges (optional)

TRY THIS...

· Swap the bacon for 50g crumbled feta.

· Use 2 teaspoons chipotle or harissa paste
  instead of smoked paprika.

METHOD:

Preheat the oven to 200°C. Lay the bacon
rashers on a baking tray with the flaked almonds
and roast for 4–6 minutes until the bacon is crisp
and the almonds lightly toasted. Break up the
bacon into pieces.

Meanwhile, cut off the broccoli florets and cut
the stalk into similar-sized pieces. Put in a pan
with a little oil and the smoked paprika. Season.
Fry over a medium heat for 5 minutes until the
broccoli is just cooked but is still very crunchy.
Remove from the heat and drizzle over the
honey, if using. Toss and set aside.

Remove the core and seeds from the peppers,
then cut into chunks.

To pack: Once cool, place the bacon, broccoli,
peppers and rocket in sections in the lunchboxes.
Garnish with the toasted flaked almonds and
tuck in a wedge of lemon, if you like.

BROCCOLI-WALNUT 'RICE' + SALMON

INGREDIENTS:

2 salmon fillets, about 150g each
3cm piece fresh ginger
rapeseed oil
2 teaspoons honey
1 medium head of broccoli (or 10 stalks
   of Tenderstem broccoli)
60g walnuts
100g chopped kale
2 teaspoons tahini

TRY THIS...

· Sprinkle with a handful of pomegranate seeds
  or 50g crumbled feta.

· Tuck in a lemon wedge to squeeze over before
  eating.

METHOD:

Preheat the oven to 180°C and boil a full kettle.
Place the salmon on a baking tray. Peel the
ginger and grate over the salmon. Mix the ginger
with a little oil and seasoning. Drizzle with honey
and bake for 12 minutes until just cooked.

Meanwhile, split the head of broccoli lengthways
in half (or take 5 of the Tenderstem stalks)
and trim the ends. Place in a pan, cover with
boiled water and add a pinch of salt. Cook for
4 minutes until al dente. Drain and rinse under
cold water.

Finely chop the rest of the broccoli. Chop the
walnuts into similar-sized pieces. Combine the
finely chopped broccoli and walnuts in a frying
pan with a little oil and seasoning, and cook
over a medium heat for 3 minutes until just soft,
stirring occasionally. Set aside.

Put the kale in a bowl and cover with boiled
water. Leave for 4 minutes, then drain and rinse
under cold water. Squeeze out any excess water
before mixing the kale with the fried broccoli and
walnut 'rice'. Stir through the tahini and a little
more oil and season well.

To pack: Spoon the 'rice' mix into the lunchboxes
and top with the broccoli pieces and whole
salmon fillets.

BROCCOLI LINGUINI WITH GREEN PESTO + PINE NUTS

INGREDIENTS:

170g linguini
olive oil
1 medium head of broccoli
½–1 teaspoon dried chilli flakes, to taste
100g baby spinach leaves
2 portions of Green Pesto *(see page 154)*
40g toasted pine nuts
50g Parmesan shavings

METHOD:

Boil a full kettle. Put the linguini in a pan with a good pinch of salt and cover with boiled water. Cook for 8–10 minutes until al dente. Drain and mix with a little olive oil to prevent sticking.

While the pasta is cooking, cut off the broccoli florets and cut the stalk into similar-sized pieces. Put the broccoli stalk pieces in a pan with a pinch of salt and cover with boiled water. Cook for 1 minute. Add the florets and cook for a further 2–3 minutes until al dente. Drain and rinse under cold water.

Heat a large pan with a splash of olive oil over a low heat. Add the chilli flakes, spinach and broccoli, turn up the heat and fry for 3 minutes. Remove from the heat and stir through the linguini and pesto.

To pack: Once cooled, spoon the pasta salad into the lunchboxes and sprinkle the pine nuts and Parmesan on top.

TRY THIS...

· For a stripped-back lunch, try without the pesto and add extra olive oil and some lemon juice.

· Add salmon. Drizzle oil over 1–2 x 150g salmon fillets and sprinkle over some dried Italian herbs or extra pesto. Bake in a 180°C oven for about 12 minutes until cooked through. Flake and stir through the pasta.

KALE

KALE PASTA SALAD WITH COCONUT-LIME DRESSING

INGREDIENTS:

200g wholemeal pasta shells
80g Tenderstem broccoli
150g chopped kale
2 portions of Coconut-lime Dressing
  (see page 153)
50g rocket

TRY THIS...

Drizzle a little oil over 2 trout fillets, sprinkle with some sesame seeds and bake in a 180°C oven for 12 minutes. Flake over the pasta salad in the lunchboxes before adding the rocket.

METHOD:

Boil a full kettle. Put the pasta in a pan with a pinch of salt and cover with boiled water. Boil for 12–15 minutes until al dente. Drain well.

While the pasta is cooking, trim the ends off the broccoli, then cut the stems in half. Place in a pan with a pinch of salt and cover with boiled water. Boil for 4–5 minutes until al dente. Drain and rinse under cold water.

Put the kale in a bowl, cover with boiled water and leave for 4–5 minutes. Drain and rinse under cold water, then squeeeze out excess water.

Combine the pasta, kale and broccoli with the coconut dressing.

To pack: Once cool, spoon the salad into the lunchboxes and place the rocket leaves on top.

KALE, BEETROOT + WALNUT HASH

INGREDIENTS:	METHOD:
2 sweet potatoes 1 red onion 4 ready-cooked and peeled beetroots 2 garlic cloves rapeseed oil 160g chopped kale 60g walnuts *Tahini dressing* 4 tablespoons tahini juice of 1 lemon, or to taste	Boil a full kettle. Peel and dice the sweet potato into 2cm chunks. Place in a pan with a pinch of salt and cover with boiled water. Simmer for 6–8 minutes until just cooked through. Drain. While the sweet potatoes are cooking, peel the onion and chop with the beetroots into 2cm chunks. Peel and finely chop the garlic. Heat a pan with a little oil and add the cooked sweet potato, beetroot and red onion. Fry over a medium heat for 5 minutes, stirring frequently. Stir through the kale, garlic and walnuts and cook for a further 5 minutes. Keep stirring. Make the dressing by mixing the tahini and lemon juice with 50ml water. Season. *To pack:* Allow the salad to cool before dividing between two lunchboxes. Pack the dressing separately.

TRY THIS… When frying the sweet potato, beetroot and onion, add 2 diced sausages or chicken fillets and fry until cooked through.

3 KALE FRITTATAS

Kale, ricotta and squash frittata

½ large butternut squash
100g chopped kale
6 eggs
4 tablespoons ricotta
20g mixed seeds

Salad
60g chopped kale (or baby kale leaves)
1 avocado
juice of ½ lemon
½ cucumber

Preheat the oven to 180°C and boil a full kettle. Peel the squash and dice into 1cm cubes. Place in a pan, cover with boiled water and add a pinch of salt. Boil for 5 minutes over a medium heat until just cooked through. Drain.

While the squash is cooking, chop the kale, then place in a bowl and cover with boiled water. Leave for 5 minutes to soften. Drain and rinse under cold water.

Crack the eggs into a bowl, add salt to taste and whisk together with a fork. Mix through the cooked squash, ricotta and kale. Season.

Wipe a large muffin tin with oil using kitchen paper. Pour the egg mix into the holes to fill them three-quarters full (you can make 6–8 frittatas). Sprinkle the seeds on top. Place in the middle of the oven and bake for 10–15 minutes until each frittata is firm in the centre. Using a spatula, loosen the sides gently, then flip out on to a wire rack to cool.

For the salad, place the kale in a bowl. Peel the avocado and cut into strips, then mix with the lemon juice to prevent browning. Cut the cucumber in half lengthways and remove the seeds with a teaspoon. Slice into half-moon shapes. Add the avocado and cucumber to the bowl and toss gently with the kale (or keep these three elements separate).

To pack: Place 3 or 4 frittatas on one side in each lunchbox with the salad alongside.

TRY THIS...

· Add chopped Parma ham or cooked chicken to the egg mix.

· Serve with a sweet chilli dressing: mix 1 tablespoon sweet chilli sauce with a splash of olive oil and the juice of ½ lemon. Pack separately.

TIP:

If you don't have a muffin tin, you can cook the frittata in an ovenproof frying pan or round tin, then cut into quarters to serve.

Kale, leek and goats' cheese frittata

200g chopped kale
1 leek
6 eggs
2 teaspoons dried oregano
coconut/olive oil
40g goats' cheese
30g mixed seeds
4 cherry tomatoes

Salad
60g crunchy mixed leaves
10 cherry tomatoes

TRY THIS...

Swap the oregano and goats' cheese for
snipped fresh chives, crumbled feta and
some smoked salmon.

Preheat the oven to 180°C and boil a full kettle.
Chop the kale, then place in a bowl and cover
with boiled water. Leave for 5 minutes to soften.
Drain and rinse under cold water.

While the kale is softening, trim the leek and
finely slice. Crack the eggs into a bowl, add the
oregano and season. Whisk together with a fork.

Heat a frying pan with a splash of oil over
a medium heat. Add the leek and cook for
3–4 minutes until soft. Add the cooked kale
and stir for a minute.

Wipe a large muffin tin with oil using kitchen
paper. Distribute the cooked kale and leek mix
equally among the cups (6–8 of them), then pour
the egg mix into the holes to fill them three-
quarters full. Sprinkle the goats' cheese on top
along with the seeds and halved cherry tomatoes.

Place in the middle of the oven and bake for
10–15 minutes until each frittata is firm in the
centre. Using a spatula, loosen the sides gently,
then flip out on to a wire rack to cool.

To pack: Place 3 or 4 frittatas on one side in
each lunchbox with the salad leaves and cherry
tomatoes alongside.

Kale, chorizo, feta and caramelised red onion frittata

200g chopped kale
60g chorizo
1 red pepper
6 eggs
40g feta
4 tablespoons ready-made caramelised red onion chutney (or make your own, *see opposite*)
20g mixed seeds
30g crunchy salad leaves

Preheat the oven to 180°C. Boil a full kettle.

Place the kale in a bowl, cover with boiled water and leave for 5 minutes. Drain and rinse under cold water, then squeeze out excess water.

Dice the chorizo. Remove the core and seeds from the red pepper. Dice half into 1cm pieces and cut the other half into 1cm-thick strips.

Crack the eggs into a bowl, add a pinch of salt and whisk together with a fork. Stir through the kale, diced red pepper, crumbled feta and red onion chutney.

Wipe a large muffin tin with oil using kitchen paper. Pour the egg mix into the holes to fill them three-quarters full (you can make 6–8 frittatas). Sprinkle the seeds on top. Place in the middle of the oven and bake for 10–15 minutes until each frittata is firm in the centre. Using a spatula, loosen the sides gently, then flip out on to a wire rack to cool.

To pack: Place 3 or 4 frittatas on one side in each lunchbox with the salad leaves and red pepper strips alongside.

TRY THIS...

Make your own red onion chutney: sweat 4 finely sliced red onions in a splash of oil over a low heat for 10 minutes until soft. Stir in 2 tablespoons sugar or honey and cook over a medium heat, stirring regularly, until the onions are slightly caramelised.

SEEDED KALE + BUTTERMILK
CHICKEN CAESAR SALAD

INGREDIENTS:

2 skinless boneless chicken breasts

rapeseed oil

1 lemon

50g mixed seeds (sesame, pumpkin
and sunflower)

200g chopped kale

1 cucumber

30g Parmesan shavings

2 portions of Buttermilk Caesar Dressing
(see page 152)

TRY THIS…

· Swap the seeds for toasted mixed nuts.
Crush them lightly before toasting to release
more nutty flavour.

· Toast some chopped rye bread with crushed
garlic and olive oil in the oven to create rye
croutons. Pack these separately to sprinkle
on the salad before eating.

METHOD:

Preheat the oven to 180°C and boil a full kettle.
Place the chicken breasts on a baking tray and
drizzle over a little oil. Zest the lemon over the
chicken and sprinkle with half of the mixed
seeds. Bake for 15–18 minutes until cooked
through. Cool.

While the chicken is in the oven, place the kale
in a bowl, cover with boiled water and leave for
5 minutes to soften; drain and rinse under cold
water.

Slice the cucumber in half lengthways, and again
in half lengthways so you have 4 strips. Remove
the watery seeds with a small knife or teaspoon.
Dice the cucumber into 1cm cubes. Toss with the
kale and Parmesan.

To pack: Spread the kale salad in the lunchboxes.
Slice the chicken at an angle into 2cm slices
and lay on top of the salad. Sprinkle over the
remaining seeds. Pack the dressing separately.

KALE + WALNUT PESTO SALAD

INGREDIENTS:

150g black quinoa
200g chopped kale
200g frozen shelled edamame beans
2 tablespoons desiccated coconut
2 portions of Kale and Walnut Pesto
  (see page 155)
4 tablespoons pomegranate seeds

TRY THIS…

Serve with a baked salmon fillet. Place 2 fillets, about 150g each, on a baking tray, sprinkle with a little oil and season with salt. Bake in a 180°C oven for 12 minutes. Leave to cool before flaking over the salad when packing.

METHOD:

Boil a full kettle. Put the quinoa in a pan, cover with boiled water and cook for 8–10 minutes. Drain and rinse under cold water. Tip into a bowl.

While the quinoa is cooking, roughly chop the kale, place in a bowl and cover with boiled water. Add a pinch of salt and leave for 5 minutes, then drain and rinse under cold water. Add to the bowl of quinoa.

Thaw the edamame in a bowl of cold water for 1–2 minutes, then drain.

Toast the coconut in a small dry pan over a medium heat until golden. Add half to the quinoa bowl; keep the rest for garnish.

When making the pesto, add a little extra oil/ water to create a loose consistency. Add the pesto to the quinoa bowl along with half of the pomegranate seeds and half the edamame beans. Toss all the ingredients together.

To pack: Spoon the salad into the lunchboxes. Sprinkle over the remaining toasted coconut, pomegranate seeds and edamame beans.

KALE RANCH SALAD

INGREDIENTS:

2 skinless boneless chicken breasts
olive oil for drizzling
4 tablespoons pumpkin seeds
2 streaky bacon rashers
200g chopped kale
1 x 340g can sweetcorn
1 tablespoon smoked paprika
2 handfuls of cherry tomatoes
2 portions of Buttermilk Caesar Dressing
  (see page 152), with extra Tabasco to taste

TRY THIS…

Use 2 corn on the cob instead of canned
sweetcorn. Place the sweetcorn in a pan, cover
with boiled water and add a pinch of salt. Simmer
over a medium heat for 6–7 minutes. Drain and
rinse under cold water. Once cool, shave the
sweetcorn kernels off the cob using a sharp knife.

METHOD:

Preheat the oven to 180°C and boil a full kettle.
Place the chicken on a baking tray. Drizzle a
little oil over the chicken and sprinkle with
half of the pumpkin seeds. Lay the bacon
on the tray alongside the chicken. Bake the
chicken for 15–18 minutes; remove the bacon
after 8–10 minutes, once golden. Cool.

While the chicken and bacon are in the oven,
place the kale in a bowl, cover with boiled water
and leave for 5 minutes to soften. Drain and
return to the bowl.

Drain the sweetcorn and place in a pan with a
little oil and the smoked paprika. Fry over a high
heat for 3–5 minutes until some bits of sweetcorn
are just crisp. Cool.

Cut the cherry tomatoes in half and add to the
bowl of kale.

Slice the chicken at an angle into 2cm slices.
Gently break up the bacon with your fingers.

To pack: Spread the kale and cherry tomatoes on
the base of the lunchboxes. Top with the fanned
sliced chicken and sprinkle over the sweetcorn,
remaining pumpkin seeds and bacon. Pack the
dressing separately.

SAUCES

BUTTERMILK CAESAR DRESSING

MAKES 4 LUNCHBOX PORTIONS

An alternative to a classic Caesar dressing, this works well on simple salads and alongside BBQ'd dishes and spicy dishes.

INGREDIENTS:

1 garlic clove
50g Parmesan
2 tablespoons finely snipped fresh chives
225ml buttermilk
4 drops of Tabasco
2 tablespoons Worcestershire sauce

METHOD:

Peel the garlic and crush into a bowl. Grate in the Parmesan. Add the remaining ingredients and whisk together with a fork. This can be kept in the fridge in an airtight container for 2–3 days.

TRY THIS...

Make it your own by mixing the chives with other soft herbs or adding extra Tabasco, or crumbling through 50g melted soft blue cheese.

Swap the buttermilk for natural yoghurt.

COCONUT-LIME DRESSING

A smooth coconut dressing with flavours that
work especially well with Asian, fish and lentil-
based dishes.

INGREDIENTS:

1 x 400ml can coconut milk
1–2 fresh green chillies
4 limes
4 tablespoons honey

METHOD:

Measure 250ml of the creamy part of the
coconut milk from the can. Pour this into a pan.
Reserve the liquid part of the coconut milk in
case you need to loosen the dressing at the end.

Finely dice the chilli (keeping or removing the
seeds, depending on how much you like heat).
Add to the pan.

Zest the limes into the pan and add the juice
too. Bring to the boil, then immediately lower
the heat and simmer for 10 minutes, stirring
occasionally. The dressing will thicken into a
syrupy consistency – stir in liquid coconut milk
if the dressing becomes too thick.

Remove from the heat and stir through the
honey. Season. This can be kept in the fridge
in an airtight container for 3–5 days. It also
freezes well for 3 months in ice-cube trays.
Thaw before using.

GREEN PESTO

MAKES 4 LUNCHBOX PORTIONS	TRY THIS…

Pestos are perfect for using up leftover herbs, salad and nuts. Pine nuts are traditional but unsalted cashews will create a similar, creamy pesto.

INGREDIENTS:

1 garlic clove (optional)
30g Parmesan
40 fresh basil leaves
60g pine nuts (or other nuts)
3 tablespoons olive oil
juice of 1–2 lemons

METHOD:

Peel the garlic (if using). Turn on a food processor and drop the garlic on to the turning blades. Grate the Parmesan and add to the processor bowl along with the basil, pine nuts, oil and 3 tablespoons water. Blitz everything together for 2 minutes until broken down.

Add lemon juice to taste plus extra water, if needed, to reach your desired texture and flavour. The pesto should not be completely smooth but should run off the spoon like a thick sauce rather than a dip. Season well.

This can be kept in the fridge in an airtight container, covered with a thin layer of olive oil, for up to a week. It also freezes well for 3 months – place in ice-cube trays for individual portions and thaw before using.

· You can omit the Parmesan and use a splash of natural yoghurt/almond milk for creaminess instead.

· Toasting the nuts will give a deeper colour and flavour.

· Swap the basil for other soft herbs such as parsley/coriander, or use a mixture.

· Add a handful of rocket for pepperiness or spinach for a rich green flavour.

· Throw in a handful of seeds.

· Experiment with different cheeses – pecorino and Manchego both work well.

· Serve leftover pesto on toast topped with an egg at breakfast, or with oatcakes or raw slices of courgette as a snack/starter.

2 MORE PESTO IDEAS

Red pepper pesto

Make the Green Pesto (*see opposite*), but add
1 jarred roasted red pepper and 5 sun-dried
tomatoes and omit the water and oil when
blitzing.

TRY THIS...

· Swap the Parmesan for feta.

· Add ½ fresh red chilli or a pinch of dried chilli
flakes for more heat.

Kale and walnut pesto

Soak 30g chopped kale in boiled water for
5 minutes, then drain and rinse in cold water.
Make the Green Pesto (*see opposite*), but use
walnuts instead of pine nuts and add the
kale when blitzing.

THAI GREEN PASTE

MAKES 4 LUNCHBOX PORTIONS

This is a powerful, fresh green Thai sauce, great
as a base for curries but also soups, or to add to
stir-fries or melt into a dressing (it is solid because
of the coconut oil, so melt in the microwave).

INGREDIENTS:

3 fresh green chillies
2cm piece fresh ginger
2 garlic cloves
1 small onion
20g fresh coriander
1 teaspoon fish sauce
2 tablespoons coconut oil
1 lemongrass stick, tough outer parts removed
1 teaspoon black pepper
1 teaspoon ground cumin
1 tablespoon ground coriander
1 lime

METHOD:

Remove the core from the chillies (and the seeds
too if you prefer). Peel the ginger and garlic.
Peel and roughly chop the onion. Place all these
prepared ingredients in a blender and add the
coriander, fish sauce, coconut oil, lemongrass and
spices. Zest the lime into the blender and add the
juice too. Blend until smooth.

Add a splash of water to loosen the paste to a thick
sauce consistency. Season with a pinch of salt.

This can be kept in the fridge in an airtight
container for 3–5 days. It also freezes well for
3 months (store in ice-cube trays so you can take
a portion out as you need it); thaw before using.

SATAY DRESSING

This recipe works as a dip, sauce or loose dressing. The consistency can be adjusted simply by adding extra water. Great on salads or with stir-fries, it also can be used as a marinade for baked fish and meat.

INGREDIENTS:

2cm piece fresh ginger
80g peanut butter (preferably smooth
    and sugar-free)
8 teaspoons soy sauce
10g picked fresh coriander leaves
2 teaspoons honey (optional)
1 fresh red chilli (optional)
zest and juice of 1–2 limes (optional)

METHOD:

Peel the ginger and drop into a blender. Add the peanut butter, soy sauce and coriander and blend until smooth. Run the machine while adding hot water in small amounts to achieve a creamy consistency.

For a sweeter sauce, add the honey. If you want a kick of heat, add the chilli. Add the lime for zing.

This can be kept in the fridge in an airtight container for 3–5 days. It also freezes well for 3 months in ice-cube trays. Thaw before using.

PEANUT TERIYAKI SAUCE

A quick, home-made version of Japanese teriyaki, this includes nuts and sesame oil for a deeper flavour.

INGREDIENTS:

20 drops of Tabasco
4 teaspoons honey
4 teaspoons toasted sesame oil
4 tablespoons soy sauce
1 tablespoon peanut butter
    (preferably smooth and sugar-free)

METHOD:

Combine all the ingredients in a small pan and simmer for 3 minutes over a high heat. Keep stirring. Allow to cool.

This can be kept in the fridge in an airtight container for 3–5 days. It also freezes well for 3 months in ice-cube trays. Thaw before using.

HUMMUS

MAKES 4 LUNCHBOX PORTIONS	TRY THIS…
A dollop of hummus is a nice addition to any salad and another way of using up fresh and tinned ingredients.	· For a classic hummus, add 1 teaspoon tahini, a pinch of ground cumin and ½ garlic clove when blitzing.
	· A handful of spinach/rocket blitzed in will give a green hummus.
INGREDIENTS:	· Stir in 3–4 tablespoons natural yoghurt to make the hummus creamier (good with spiced food or eggs at breakfast).
1 x 400g can chickpeas juice of 1 lemon 2 tablespoons olive oil	· Give the hummus a Middle Eastern twist with 2 teaspoons harissa paste.
	· Blitz in the flesh from 1 avocado and a handful of fresh coriander.
METHOD:	· Add 5 sun-dried tomatoes and a handful of fresh basil leaves when blitzing.
Drain and rinse the chickpeas, then tip into a food processor and add the lemon, oil and 1 tablespoon water. Blitz until smooth. If needed, add extra water to loosen to the desired consistency. Season to taste.	· For a hot Mexican-style hummus, add a handful of jarred jalapeño chillies and fresh lime juice when blitzing.
This can be kept in the fridge in an airtight container for 3–5 days.	· Finish with a tablespoon of any of our pestos (*see pages 154–155*).

2 MORE HUMMUS IDEAS

Beetroot hummus	*Red pepper and butter bean hummus*
1 x 400g can chickpeas, drained and rinsed juice of 1 lemon 3 ready-cooked and peeled beetroots 2 tablespoons olive oil 1 tablespoon water	1 x 400g can butter beans juice of 1 lemon 1 jarred roasted red pepper (4 pieces) 2 tablespoons olive oil 1 tablespoon water
Follow the method for Hummus (above).	Follow the method for Hummus (above).

INDEX

10 9 8 7 6 5 4 3 2 1

Ebury Press, an imprint of Ebury Publishing,
20 Vauxhall Bridge Road,
London, SW1V 2SA

Ebury Press is part of the Penguin Random House
group of companies whose addresses can be found
at global.penguinrandomhouse.com

First published by Ebury Press in 2017

www.penguin.co.uk

A CIP catalogue record for this book is available
from the British Library

Design: Louise Evans

ISBN: 9781785035296

Printed and bound in China by Toppan Leefung

Penguin Random House is committed to a sustainable
future for our business, our readers and our planet.
This book is made from Forest Stewardship Council®
certified paper.

ACKNOWLEDGEMENTS

We'd like to thank everyone who has helped
us at Lunch BXD and on this book. Our parents
Rebecca & Ivan and Kate & Mark, David, (thank
you for your on going patience, support and
guidance), Rach (you are a constant inspiration
to me, thank you for your never-failing support,
love, encouragement and for donning chef
whites in times of need! –*Anna*), Kate (we never
would have begun this adventure without you),
Freya and Courtney (our dream team), Moira,
Fred, Hannah Struve (for lending us her beautiful
ceramics), Celia, Kerry, Jess, Laura, Barney and
everyone who ordered one of our lunch boxes
and supported our Lunch BXD adventure.